T0361711

ESPECIALLY FOR

....

FROM

....

DATE

....

smart start devotions

FOR YOUNG WOMEN

RENÉE SANFORD

smart start devotions

FOR YOUNG WOMEN

WISDOM AND INSPIRATION FOR NAVIGATING ADULTHOOD

28 Weeks of Readings Plus Interactive "Life Maps"

BARBOUR
PUBLISHING

Printed in China.

Introduction

In God's Word, Proverbs pictures Wisdom as a woman: "Blessed are those who listen to me, watching daily at my doors, waiting at my doorway. For those who find me find life and receive favor from the LORD" (Proverbs 8:34–35 NIV). *Smart Start Devotions for Young Women* offers applied biblical wisdom in abundance.

This book features twenty-eight weekly themed introductions plus related devotional readings for five days a week (Monday through Friday). It also features two-page "Life Map" spreads that you can fill out to help you with that week's focused devotional time. Through the 140 entries and accompanying life maps, you will be encouraged and guided to grow in the varied arenas of your life: faith, family, finances, work, health, and more.

Smart Start Devotions for Young Women will guide you into a more intentional life—one that honors God and benefits you and others for all time to come.

Why not make this your best year ever? Take Wisdom up on her invitation. Watch God change you and bless others through your life!

Whatever you do, work heartily, as for the Lord and not for men, knowing that from the Lord you will receive the inheritance as your reward. You are serving the Lord Christ.
COLOSSIANS 3:23–24 ESV

WEEK 1
Faith Basics

My husband received his first life map from his father. The older man said, "David, there are no rules. Don't obey anyone. Don't even obey me." David rejected that advice and instead responded to the Lord and Savior who created him, loved him, died for his sins, rose again, and asked him to follow wholeheartedly for the rest of his life. I'm so glad David said, "Yes!"

Thankfully, my parents gave me a life map based on God's Word. Life hasn't always been easy, but I was saved a multitude of griefs because I too trusted Jesus and followed His path. I learned about life and how it really works.

Think of this book as your own God-focused life map. It's a collection of devotionals to impart applied wisdom day after day. We'll start with Faith Basics for two weeks. Then we'll cover prayer, the Bible, fellowship, family, hospitality, God's will, work, rest, recreation, entertainment, personal improvement, fitness, travel, finances, giving back, and goal setting for a week or two each. We'll end with one final week focused on who God is in our lives.

I hope you resonate with these Smart Start devotions at every turn.

Enjoy the adventure!

Now faith is confidence in what we hope for and assurance about what we do not see.

Hebrews 11:1 NIV

8

Monday

THE CREATOR AND HIS CREATION

By faith we understand that the universe was formed at God's command, so that what is seen was not made out of what was visible.
Hebrews 11:3 niv

Read the Bible from the very beginning and you soon discover that God calls Himself "the Lord God, Creator of heaven and earth." He could simply speak and create the whole universe.

While followers of Christ may disagree about when and exactly how that happened, the bedrock foundation of belief in God is acknowledging and worshipping Him as Creator. As our Maker, and the Maker of this world, God alone has authority over our lives.

We are enraptured by stunning sunsets, pristine lakes, majestic mountains, or the glory of a star-filled sky. Feelings of transcendence rightly have only one place to go—up in worship of the one who brought each creature, each wonder, into being.

Lord, I thank You for who You are and for all You have made. Sometimes the vistas here on earth take my breath away. The night sky provokes even more awe. All because of You!

Tuesday

GOD'S LIFE BREATHED INTO HUMANITY

Then the LORD God formed a man from the dust
of the ground and breathed into his nostrils the
breath of life, and the man became a living being.
GENESIS 2:7 NIV

The Lord God spoke the heavens and earth into existence. Then He formed Adam from the dust and crafted Eve from a rib of Adam's side. While every living creature sprang to life at God's command, God breathed His very life into the first two humans. They gained not just physical life, but spiritual life.

We recognize that many animals (certainly our pets) experience emotions—but having God's breath of life (actually being made in God's image, Genesis 1:26) means we were created to connect with Him. This is a depth of existence no animal can ever experience.

No wonder scripture teaches that each human life is a gift from God—a gift to be cherished and treasured.

How will I live this human life? Will I respond to my Creator and live the life He's given me? Will I treasure and protect other human beings as made in God's image, no matter who they are?

*Lord, I thank You for who You are and for breathing
Your life into me. You designed me to know, love,
serve, and enjoy You forever. I'm happy to do so!*

Wednesday
GOD APPEARS ON EARTH

"For God so loved the world that he gave his one
and only Son [Jesus Christ], that whoever believes
in him shall not perish but have eternal life."
JOHN 3:16 NIV

God didn't make Adam and Eve only to send them into the wilderness. They didn't have to make a life for themselves. No, God planted a garden for them to cultivate, then met with them in the "magic hour" of the early evenings to enjoy their company.

Throughout the Old Testament (the Hebrew Bible), God kept visiting earth. Sometimes He appeared in human- or angel-like form. Sometimes he appeared in storms and whirlwinds, lights and fire.

The New Testament describes how God made His climactic visit to earth in the form of His Son, Jesus Christ. The Gospels—Matthew, Mark, Luke, and John—tell us the beautiful story of Jesus' life, ministry, teaching, miracles, betrayal, death, burial, and resurrection and His promise to return one day.

God was delighted to be with the first two people who walked the earth. I can't wait to be embraced by the Lord and walk with Him for the first time. How about you?

Lord, thank You for appearing on earth
so often and at such great cost to Your Son.
I eagerly wait for You to come again.

Thursday

THE FALL INTO EVIL

*"The thief comes only to steal and kill and destroy.
I came that they may have life and have it abundantly."*
JOHN 10:10 ESV

If God desires our presence so much, why does He seem so far away? Why don't we hear His voice clearly?

The Bible describes the day that Eve listened to Satan's deceptive words, disregarding God's one prohibition to eat fruit from the Tree of the Knowledge of Good and Evil. Adam ate the fruit with her, and together they plunged into the darkness of separation from God. Human beings truly experienced the terrible knowledge of good and evil. And every person born after inherited both the life God breathed into our first parents and the burden of shame they chose.

In His mercy, God clothed Adam and Eve in their shame. His curse on the serpent assured them that a Savior would come and rescue them from the enemy (Genesis 3:15).

On this earth, Satan wants to steal from, kill, and destroy the precious people God created. But Jesus is the Savior who paid the price for human sin, conquered the death we deserved, and offers everyone abundant life.

*Lord, thank You for rescuing Adam and Eve
and sending Your Son, Jesus Christ, to die
for me and my sins. Help me to see through
Satan's every ploy to ruin my life.*

Friday

TIME AND ETERNITY

*Fight the good fight of the faith. Take hold
of the eternal life to which you were called
when you made your good confession in
the presence of many witnesses.*
1 TIMOTHY 6:12 NIV

God doesn't give us a thousand-dollar gold coin every time we say "Yes!" to His Word, His will, and His ways. No, He has something far more valuable reserved for us in heaven. The Bible describes our reward as something real and tangible, a "weight" of glory (2 Corinthians 4:17 NKJV). What does God reward? Our faith. Trusting Him is more valuable to God than the purest gold (1 Peter 1:7).

Mathematically, infinity and eternity eclipse seventy-five trillion dollars and a hundred billion years. To understand this is paramount to living wisely in our finite, time-bound world. As precious as this life is, it is only the foretaste of a life that will go on forever. As brief as this life is, it can create profound impact for eternity.

During this weekend, be sure to complete the first of the twenty-eight Life Maps in this book. Completing them is the key to mining the full benefit from this adventure. Enjoy!

Lord, show me how each Faith Basic applies to me at this stage of my life. And please bless me, Lord, I pray.

Date: ....

Lord, this week we've considered powerful truths that appear in the opening pages of scripture and that reverberate through the rest of the Bible. Most of all, how great You are!

5 TOPICS COVERED THIS WEEK:

Monday: the Creator and His creation

Tuesday: God's life breathed into humanity

Wednesday: God appears on earth

Thursday: the fall into evil

Friday: time and eternity

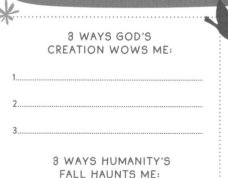

3 WAYS GOD'S CREATION WOWS ME:

1. ....

2. ....

3. ....

3 WAYS HUMANITY'S FALL HAUNTS ME:

1. ....

2. ....

3. ....

How I want to respond to these truths:

....

....

....

....

....

....

....

....

....

LORD, HERE'S WHAT'S GOING ON IN MY LIFE RIGHT NOW. . .

OTHER THINGS I NEED TO
SHARE WITH YOU, LORD. . .

Lord, when it comes to this
new life map, I need to. . .

Without faith it is
impossible to please
God, because anyone
who comes to him must
believe that he exists and
that he rewards those
who earnestly seek him.
HEBREWS 11:6 NIV

Thank You, Lord, for
hearing my prayers
and for helping
me take action!
AMEN.

WEEK 2
More Faith Basics

The first week we considered the Faith Basics of the Creator and creation, of God's life breathed into human beings, of the Lord's appearances, of the fall into evil, and of the vast and weighty difference between time and eternity.

This second week—before we begin considering each major sphere of life for six months—we have five more Faith Basics to cover. We will consider our Lord Jesus Christ, our faith's good works, the certainty of God's judgment, knowing what's true and what's not, and going deeper into God's Word, the Bible.

The more we learn from God's Word (and the more we trust the Lord Himself), the more we will enjoy His good hand of blessing in our lives. Not the "everything goes my way" kind of blessings, but the true gifts of peace with God and others, belonging and significance, hope for the future and much, much more.

May your sense of forgiveness and belonging increase this week!

> *"Receive forgiveness of sins and a place among those who are sanctified by faith in me [Jesus Christ]."*
>
> ACTS 26:18 NIV

Monday

OUR LORD JESUS CHRIST

Through [Jesus Christ] you believe in God,
who raised him from the dead and glorified
him, and so your faith and hope are in God.
1 PETER 1:21 NIV

Certain decisions you make can change the whole trajectory of your life. First and foremost, for now and eternity, is the decision to become a wholehearted follower of Jesus Christ.

It's not enough to believe Jesus died for our sins on a Roman cross, was buried, and rose again from the grave three days later. The Lord calls us to put our entire faith, trust, hope, and love in God. Jesus says to us as He said to His first disciples, "Come, follow me" (Matthew 4:19 NIV).

David and I had been friends for many years, so from the very beginning of our dating relationship we couldn't imagine the rest of our lives without each other. Similarly, we should never imagine our lives without Jesus at the forefront. Because He reigns supreme over heaven and earth, we will gladly follow Him through joys and sorrows, pain and delight.

Lord, thank You for bringing me to faith in You and changing the whole trajectory of my life—here on earth and for eternity. I can't imagine my life without You.

Tuesday
OUR FAITH'S GOOD WORKS

*We keep on praying for you, asking our God
to enable you to live a life worthy of his call.
May he give you the power to accomplish all the
good things your faith prompts you to do.*
2 THESSALONIANS 1:11 NLT

When David and I finally admitted our love for each other and began a committed relationship, our thoughts, words, and actions changed. We couldn't wait to spend hours together, even though it usually meant a three-hour drive. We spent as much time as we could on the phone (before cell service) and wrote long letters (before email).

In every way, we wanted to demonstrate our love to each other. We didn't just daydream, but spent real time and money on travel, gifts, and making special memories. Not to earn each other's love, but because our love and commitment propelled us to do so.

Similarly, David and I want to demonstrate our love for the Lord. The secret? God's power in us, prompting us to do good. That is, more good works for His glory, honor, and praise. May that be your desire too!

*Lord, I want to do even more for You. Thank You
for Your power at work in and through me. Please
prompt me to do something more for You today.*

Wednesday

WHAT'S TRUE AND WHAT'S NOT

We demolish arguments and every pretension that sets itself up against the knowledge of God, and we take captive every thought to make it obedient to Christ.
2 CORINTHIANS 10:5 NIV

The devil knows a lot of languages, but only one way to speak. And not just a lie here and there, but a rushing torrent of flaming darts designed to knock us off our feet. We fight back in two ways.

First, we identify Satan's lies and demolish them with God's truth. Then we carefully examine every new thought that comes our way. Our key question: Does this thought accurately reflect Jesus Christ and align with God's Word?

Secondly, we let our minds be transformed in keeping with the verse above, Romans 12:1–2, and other scriptures.

The enemy never tires of attacking our hearts and minds, so we must always be alert. But we can be confident that God's truth and justice will always prevail.

Lord, give me strength to keep fighting Satan's lies and test every new thought that comes my way. Speak to me, lead me, guide me. Keep me fighting the good fight, I pray.

Thursday

THE CERTAINTY OF GOD'S JUDGMENT

It is appointed for man to die once,
and after that comes judgment.
HEBREWS 9:27 ESV

Because David feared my possible rejection of his love, he hesitated—I finally had to say first that I loved him! Two years later, he asked me to marry him, without any fear. He knew I already had judged him worthy of my lifelong love.

When we put our faith in Jesus Christ and are born into God's family, we can live without fear because we are already judged worthy. Not because of what we have done, but because of Jesus.

Satan's biggest lies question whether or not we can trust God to be both good and just. The devil paints a picture of God as a feeble old man unsure of what to do. But when we appear before God someday—as each person will—we can be sure that His judgments will be true. He knows everything (Psalm 147:5)—especially those who belong to His Son, Jesus, by faith. We can trust God to do what is right.

Lord, I thank You that I can trust You fully—
especially what You will do and say on judgment
day. I know I am covered by Jesus' sacrifice. Amen!

Friday
GOD'S WORD, THE BIBLE

*All Scripture is breathed out by God and profitable
for teaching, for reproof, for correction, and for
training in righteousness, that the man of God
may be complete, equipped for every good work.*
2 TIMOTHY 3:16–17 ESV

Shortly after David and I started dating, we supplemented visits and Saturday morning phone calls with lots of full-length letters. David went to his college mailbox eagerly each day. Then, one day, it was empty. And not just for one day, but for the next four. David was crushed. By day five, he had resigned himself to serving God as a single missionary and dying young.

Then they appeared: six letters that I had written six different days, but which the postal service delivered at the same time.

Thankfully, God's letters to us—the books of the Bible—are all available, all the time. His Word tells us everything we need to know for life and good works.

If you want real life, stop searching elsewhere; dive deeper into God's holy and inspired Word. The Creator and sustainer of the universe speaks loud and clear if only we have the ears to hear.

*Lord, thanks for giving us Your Word. I want to
learn it better in the weeks and years to come.*

Date: ....

Lord, how wonderful that I need not worry whether I
should trust You. You have promised and shown a deep,
deep love for me. You are righteous in all You say and do!

5 TOPICS COVERED THIS WEEK:

Monday: our Lord Jesus Christ

Tuesday: our faith's good works

Wednesday: the certainty of God's judgment

Thursday: what's true and what's not

Friday: God's Word, the Bible

3 WAYS GOD'S LOVE INSPIRES ME:

1 ....

2 ....

3 ....

3 WAYS SATAN'S LIES HAVE TRIPPED ME UP:

1 ....

2 ....

3 ....

How I want to respond to these truths:

LORD, HERE'S WHAT'S GOING ON IN MY LIFE RIGHT NOW. . .

OTHER THINGS I NEED TO
SHARE WITH YOU, LORD. . .

Lord, when it comes to this
new life map, I need to. . .

In the gospel the
righteousness of God is
revealed—a righteousness
that is by faith from
first to last, just as it is
written: "The righteous
will live by faith."
ROMANS 1:17 NIV

Thank You, Lord, for
hearing my prayers
and for helping
me take action!
AMEN.

WEEK 3
Praying for Yourself

Does it seem selfish to pray for yourself? You and I may choose to pray often for others (which is great!) but feel less comfortable talking to God about our own needs. But that is appropriate prayer too.

God repeatedly invites us to ask Him for things we need. Jesus asked people, "What do you want me to do for you?" In fact, not asking is wrong. God was angry with King Ahab when he refused to ask for anything (Isaiah 7:10–14). When King Asa refused to pray about his own serious illness, he died (2 Chronicles 16:12). In both cases, their blatant unwillingness to pray revealed a lack of love for God, and failure to trust Him.

Yes, we will experience God's power answering our prayers for other people, but He also wants us to experience His power to answer our prayers, meet our needs, and change our lives.

This week we will take time to ponder what it means to pray for ourselves—and do it!

> *"What do you want me to do for you?" Jesus asked him. The blind man said, "Rabbi, I want to see."*
>
> MARK 10:51 NIV

Monday

EXPERIENCE YOURSELF AS GOD DOES

*"The Father himself loves you dearly because you
love me and believe that I came from God."*
JOHN 16:27 NLT

When I come to the Lord to pray for myself, I must first experience myself as He does. Do I imagine God hears me as a bothersome interruption or an unwelcome visitor? If so, I will hesitate to go to God with my needs, my hurts, and my deepest desires. Then again, if I know that I am God's beloved child, I'll trust He hears my voice with delight. He says: "Pull up a chair! I was waiting for you. I want to hear everything!"

When I pray for myself, I begin thanking God for who He is and who He made me to be. I don't ask for anything, I just revel—as any woman does when she is deeply loved. Like an infant looking into its mother's eyes, I fix my eyes on Jesus. . .and His love draws me closer to His heart.

If you haven't experienced yourself as God does, ask Him to make this your reality. It's a prayer He delights to answer!

*Lord, before anything else, I want to
know and experience who I am to You.
Then I can enjoy Your love for me.*

Tuesday
BARE YOUR SOUL

*I cry out to the LORD; I plead for the LORD's
mercy. I pour out my complaints before
him and tell him all my troubles.*
PSALM 142:1–2 NLT

When I pray for myself, I can bare my soul completely to God. God can handle any emotions I'm experiencing and any questions I bring. He isn't uneasy or afraid or caught off guard.

In the Bible, David constantly poured out his frustrations, anger, sorrow, and longings to God—and we read them today as the psalms. David's strong words may make us feel uncomfortable, but their place in scripture proves that we too can be completely honest with God. We can rant and rave and ask any question—though, like Job, we may be stunned by God's direct answers.

Rebekah asked God directly why her twin babies were wrestling so hard in her womb. Hannah begged God with tears when she was mistreated, misunderstood, and desperate for a baby. Paul begged God three times to remove a painful "thorn" in his life.

God already knows our hearts, but He wants to hear our cries. He also wants to hear our trust in Him. No one but God can be trusted to understand and rescue us.

*Lord, I open my heart to You—no hiding,
no pretending. I know that I can trust You completely.*

Wednesday
INVITE GOD'S WORK IN YOUR LIFE

> Search me, God, and know my heart;
> test me and know my anxious thoughts.
> See if there is any offensive way in me,
> and lead me in the way everlasting.
> PSALM 139:23–24 NIV

As my Maker, God knows me fully and intimately. He understands me more completely than I will ever understand myself. As human beings, we only know ourselves in a very limited fashion—I don't know most of my own motives and faults, or I easily overlook them. When I come to God, I need to slow down.

Praying for myself starts best with introspection. I ask God not only to forgive me for my daily sins, but also for the patterns of disobedience, unkindness, or selfishness in my life. I ask the Holy Spirit to reveal these to me and to change me from the inside out. When the Spirit answers, His voice will be one of conviction about specific sin or needed change—not the enemy's lies that say I'm hopeless and I'll never be forgiven.

The answer to my prayers for myself is God—the only one who can bring about the change (the "spiritual fruit") that comes from following the Lord.

*Lord, show me who I am and where I
need to change. Then bring growth in my
life that makes me more like Jesus.*

Thursday

PRAY WHEN ANXIOUS AND DEPRESSED

*Enter his gates with thanksgiving, and his courts
with praise! Give thanks to him; bless his name!*
PSALM 100:4 ESV

How often have you lain awake at night, your mind swirling with anxiety and your spirit crushed with depression? Perhaps you cry out to the Lord in prayer, but the thoughts keep coming—you can't turn them off. The morning may bring sunshine, but you wear a heavy blanket of worry all day. How do you pray when your spirit is dark—and God hasn't promised an easy fix?

During these times, two railings have kept me steady on the path of prayer: thankfulness and God's Word. When I'm awake and my thoughts won't stop, I fill my mind with worship for who God is and thankfulness for what He's done. And when a troubling situation or person comes to mind, I have a verse ready to recite. To name two favorites: "Love one another fervently with a pure heart" (1 Peter 1:22 NKJV) and "The LORD is close to the brokenhearted" (Psalm 34:18 NIV).

Worship settles my mind and fills my spirit. Scripture brings new joy and life to my soul.

*Lord, I will fill my mind with thoughts of You
and Your Word. . .and You will give me life.*

Friday

MAKE REQUESTS

"Then you will know that I am the LORD;
those who hope in me will not be disappointed."
ISAIAH 49:23 NIV

You've walked through God's gates with thanksgiving. You've prayed for the Lord to search your heart. You've asked Him to change you from the inside out.

What else is on your heart and mind? Ask the Lord to respond to each concern in a specific, detailed manner. Then watch for God's answers. Don't rush by and miss them! When we experience God's specific answers to our prayers, our faith and trust deepen.

For many years, I hesitated to ask God for specific personal needs—I didn't want to put Him in the position of disappointing me. In time, though, I learned that God's "no" was also an answer, one that meant He would give me something better. I began to look for the "other" answers He was giving me instead.

When praying for yourself, find and quote a scripture or two. That way, you'll have the right words to express your needs and desires. You'll know you are praying in God's will. And the very words you pray will change and strengthen you.

Lord, please show me Your goodness and
power by answering my prayers for my needs.
Increase my faith as I see Your good work in my life.

Date: _____

Lord, thank You for making me Your beloved child. I'm so glad You hear my voice with delight and say: "Pull up a chair! I was waiting for you. I want to hear everything!"

5 TOPICS COVERED THIS WEEK:

Monday: experience yourself as God does
Tuesday: bare your soul
Wednesday: invite God's work in your life
Thursday: pray when anxious and depressed
Friday: make requests

3 WAYS PRAYING PERSONALLY CHANGES ME:

1. ....
2. ....
3. ....

3 WAYS PRAYING SPECIFICALLY CONCERNS ME:

1. ....
2. ....
3. ....

How I want to respond to these truths:

....
....
....
....
....
....
....
....
....

LORD, HERE'S WHAT'S GOING ON IN MY LIFE RIGHT NOW. . .

OTHER THINGS I NEED TO
SHARE WITH YOU, LORD. . .

Lord, when it comes to this
new life map, I need to. . .

"Ask and it will be given
to you; seek and you will
find; knock and the door
will be opened to you."
MATTHEW 7:7 NIV

Thank You, Lord, for
hearing my prayers
and for helping
me take action!
AMEN.

31

WEEK 4
Praying for Others

The apostle Paul constantly told others that he was praying for them, and he meant it! Like Paul, you can thank God for friends, family, people in ministry and government. You can pray for God's protection, and that He will greatly use these people in their sphere of influence. You can pray for their specific needs, and that they will see God's answers in whatever form they come.

When you say you will pray for someone, do it! And do it right then, before you forget. Better yet, pray with the person so they can hear your intercession for them.

I've had the deep privilege of being the subject of earnest praying by my friends and family, even by people I don't know personally. Whether I was in a foreign city or sitting beside someone's hospital bed, I knew that other people's prayers were carrying me through. I want to bless others with that same kind of prayer.

> *We always thank God, the Father of our Lord Jesus Christ, when we pray for you, because we have heard of your faith in Christ Jesus and the love you have for all God's people.*
> COLOSSIANS 1:3–4 NIV

Monday

PRAY FOR YOUR CHRISTIAN FRIENDS

> With this in mind, we constantly pray for you, that our
> God may make you worthy of his calling, and that by
> his power he may bring to fruition your every desire
> for goodness and your every deed prompted by faith.
>
> 2 THESSALONIANS 1:11 NIV

Do you have the gift of giving? Do you love shopping to find just the perfect item for a friend or family member? I don't have that gift—but I wish I did. Recently, though, I realized that praying for my friends was like entering the most magnificent gift shop with an unlimited line of credit. I often visualize going into God's storage room of blessings and asking Him to give bountiful gifts to those I love.

Can't think of a particular gift to give in prayer? Choose a scripture to pray for your friends—one verse per person or a single verse for a whole group. What better way to have the "right" words and pray in God's will! I recently wrote out all of the apostle Paul's prayers for his Thessalonian brothers and sisters, and each week texted a verse to my friends. Always remember that the word of God is "alive and powerful" (Hebrews 4:12 NLT).

*Lord, I thank You for all the prayers that
others have lifted up on my behalf through the
years. I want to pray more often for them.*

Tuesday
PRAY FOR YOUR COLLEAGUES

With this in mind, we constantly pray for you,
that our God may make you worthy of his calling.
2 THESSALONIANS 1:11 NIV

A friend once asked me if it is okay to pray for unbelievers. I answered, "Yes!" God gives many gifts, such as sunshine and rain, to everyone. And our prayers invite Him into non-believers' lives.

Maybe you've never thought about praying for work colleagues. But they are very important people. For better or worse, we spend most of our waking hours with them.

Once I've gotten to know coworkers well enough, I will let them know that I am praying for them in particular situations, whether for work or family or other issues. And they generally appreciate it. One colleague, introducing me to a new employee, said, "Renée will even pray for you!"

Don't forget to pray for your Christian colleagues too. First, ask God to show you who they are. Second, pray for their success and for their good witness. Third, consider inviting them to pray together for your workplace.

Even if you don't tell people you are praying for them (though I suggest you do!), your prayers will make a difference.

Lord, I see these people every day; some I
know very well. Make their work successful.
Use me to bless them and show them Jesus.

Wednesday

PRAY FOR YOUR CHURCH'S LEADERS

*Pray also for me, that whenever I speak,
words may be given me so that I will fearlessly
make known the mystery of the gospel.*
EPHESIANS 6:19 NIV

Who works at your church? The staff may include both women and men in leadership, both in shepherding and support roles. My church has five full- and part-time staff. My daughter's church has fifty. The important thing isn't the number of staff but who's praying regularly for them.

Your church staff may be surprised when you ask them how you can pray for them. They often hear complaints when they don't meet everyone's expectations, so what a gift to be told, "I'm praying for you!"

Praying for people develops our emotional connections and increases our compassion. It's much harder to be unkindly critical of those for whom you pray. Knowing and regularly praying for the staff and their responsibilities allows you to come to God with specific requests—and perhaps to go back to your leadership with more helpful suggestions!

Praying for your church leadership develops unity—and God delights in unity among His children. What great things God will do when you pray.

*Lord, help me to know my church's staff and their
needs—and then pray specifically for each one.*

Thursday
PRAY FOR GOVERNMENT LEADERS

> I urge you, first of all, to pray for all people.
> Ask God to help them; intercede on their
> behalf, and give thanks for them. Pray this
> way for kings and all who are in authority
> so that we can live peaceful and quiet
> lives marked by godliness and dignity.
> 1 TIMOTHY 2:1–2 NLT

Most people recoil at political posts on social media—unless they agree, of course! If Paul's words to Timothy were a tweet, however, they would apply to everyone, people on either side of the aisle.

Pray for those who have the authority to impact your nation and your community. Pray that they will have correct and helpful information, wise counselors, and insight as they to make decisions.

Pray for God to raise up leaders—elected and otherwise—who will bring about much good for our country. Remember Mothers Against Drunk Driving? Untold thousands of lives were saved, and a cultural value shifted.

Pray for God's Kingdom to advance, no matter what political party is in control. Because God is King over all nations, praying for our leaders is an even greater privilege than voting for them.

*Lord, when I'm tempted to complain about political
leaders, remind me to ask You to help them
govern. May I live a godly life for Your glory.*

Friday

PRAY FOR GOD'S PEOPLE EVERYWHERE

*Stay alert and be persistent in your
prayers for all believers everywhere.*
EPHESIANS 6:18 NLT

Prayer is the most powerful impact you and I will ever have on the world. I often am humbled to know that God uses my prayers to touch, bless, and change people continents away.

I pray by name for missionaries, but I also pray for the churches and communities where they work. Through Compassion International, our family sponsors an eleven-year-old Ethiopian girl, Betselot. We pray regularly for her, her family and church, her city and country. I don't pray for every country around the world, but that's okay. You and I can focus on several countries where we know people or where God leads our hearts. Listen to world news with a heart to pray for the people who are impacted.

Those who minister to persecuted believers around the world tell us that these brothers and sisters plead with us to pray for them. Pray for their protection, endurance, witness, and families.

We may never serve the Lord overseas, but our prayers can reach around the world and make a difference.

*Lord, please help me to pray for my Christian
brothers and sisters everywhere. Today, show
me a nation I can emphasize in my prayers.*

Date: ....

Lord, I'm so thankful and glad that my prayers
make a difference for my friends and acquaintances
and even people around the world.

5 TOPICS COVERED THIS WEEK:

Monday: pray for your Christian friends
Tuesday: pray for your colleagues
Wednesday: pray for your church's leaders
Thursday: pray for government leaders
Friday: pray for God's people everywhere

3 WAYS PRAYING FOR OTHERS ENERGIZES ME:

1. ....

2. ....

3. ....

3 WAYS PRAYING FOR OTHERS DRAINS ME:

1. ....

2. ....

3. ....

How I want to respond to these truths:

....

....

....

....

....

....

....

....

....

....

LORD, HERE'S WHAT'S GOING ON IN MY LIFE RIGHT NOW. . .

OTHER THINGS I NEED TO
SHARE WITH YOU, LORD. . .

Lord, when it comes to this
new life map, I need to. . .

Pray for all people.
Ask God to help them;
intercede on their behalf,
and give thanks for them.
1 TIMOTHY 2:1 NLT

Thank You, Lord, for
hearing my prayers
and for helping
me take action!
AMEN.

39

WEEK 5
Bible Reading

Certain decisions can change the whole trajectory of your life. Here are three positive ones:

First, to become a wholehearted follower of Jesus Christ. Second, to know yourself and become the "right" woman before finding and marrying the "right" man. Third, to read God's Word, the Bible, each day. Whether it's five minutes or an hour, your life will be shaped by this consistent time listening to what God has to say.

When I was nine, while attending one church, I began attending a Bible memory club at another. My parents soon realized I was growing spiritually more than they were, so we all began to attend this church where the Bible was clearly taught. Not only that, everyone was encouraged to read (and obey) God's Word. Reading the Bible became part of my daily life, shaped me into who I am, and guided me as I made major decisions.

Have you considered making the decision to read the Bible daily? I hope you will do so today!

Instruct the wise and they will be wiser still; teach the righteous and they will add to their learning. The fear of the LORD is the beginning of wisdom, and knowledge of the Holy One is understanding. For through wisdom your days will be many, and years will be added to your life.

PROVERBS 9:9–11 NIV

Monday

BEFORE YOU READ THE BIBLE

*"I have not departed from the commands of
[God's] lips; I have treasured the words of
his mouth more than my daily bread."*
JOB 23:12 NIV

When I open my Bible each day, I already have three attitudes in place. First is reverence for the Lord God, Creator of heaven and earth, and the true author of scripture. The higher my regard for the Lord, the greater benefits I'll enjoy as I read His Word.

Second is respect for the Bible itself. This book was written with the Holy Spirit's inspiration by forty individuals over the course of sixteen hundred years. Thousands of other people copied, distributed, and preserved each book of the Bible. Other thousands translated it into the world's languages today. People may disagree about meanings of words and verses, but God has given us His message in the Bible for us to obey. We can trust that.

Third is repentance of any known sin in my life before I start reading the Bible. I want the author of scripture to speak to me freely—and I ask Him to remove any barriers so I can hear Him clearly.

*Lord, I thank You for providing Your Word in
English. Please speak to me as I read it!*

Tuesday

READING THE BIBLE FOR THE FIRST TIME

They read from the Book of the Law of God,
making it clear and giving the meaning so that
the people understood what was being read.
NEHEMIAH 8:8 NIV

The first time my husband, David, read the Joseph story in Genesis, he couldn't believe how harshly it started out. David was relieved when Joseph was released from slavery and prison. He cheered when Joseph rose in power in Egypt, second only to Pharaoh.

My husband wasn't surprised that Joseph hid his identity when his brothers came to Egypt—the brothers who had originally sold him into slavery. They wanted to buy grain for their families experiencing famine back in Canaan. David smiled when Joseph spoke harshly to the men.

By the time David started Genesis 45, he sensed Joseph's revenge was right around the corner. In the climactic moment, when Joseph revealed his true identity, David expected the brothers to be slaughtered like pigs—but instead, Joseph forgave them. David broke down and wept. After all they had done to Joseph years earlier, David didn't see that coming.

When you read the Bible, read to learn—ask questions, consult study notes. But also read to be moved emotionally. These are stories of real people who experienced God in their lives. God invites you to experience Him too.

Lord, please move me as I read Your Word.

Wednesday

HOW DO I START READING THE BIBLE?

So then faith comes by hearing,
and hearing by the word of God.
ROMANS 10:17 NKJV

Made a pledge to read the Bible daily? Here are steps to help you:

1. Set a goal, for example, to read from Genesis 1 to Revelation 22 in a year. Then select a personal reward for accomplishing that goal.

2. Divide and conquer. You can finish the entire Bible in twelve months by reading fifteen minutes at a shot, roughly three chapters a day. Can't make it every day? Then read twenty minutes (about four chapters) five days a week.

3. Read with your head and heart. If you don't understand something, it's okay. But as you read, focus on what's clear. Look for (a) examples to heed, (b) truths to believe, and (c) commands to obey.

4. Pick a favorite verse to make your own. My husband and I chose Psalm 34:3 as a life verse for our marriage. I often reread a verse or passage each day that reflects my experience and speaks to my heart for particular seasons of life.

Lord, I thank You that reading the Bible
becomes easier with time. Thanks for the
privilege I have to read it daily.

Thursday

CHOOSE A BIBLE READING PLAN

Jesus answered, "It is written: 'Man shall
not live on bread alone, but on every word
that comes from the mouth of God.'"
MATTHEW 4:4 NIV

The one way not to read the Bible is to open it randomly and jump into a passage. I suppose it's better than nothing—but surely we can do better than that!

Here are four much better options:

1. Read highlights from every book of the Bible. You can digest important excerpts from Genesis to Revelation in two months.

2. Read highlights about every important person from Adam to Zechariah. In four months' time, you can become acquainted with the entire Who's Who of scripture.

3. Read the whole Bible from Genesis to Revelation. As we saw earlier, it takes only fifteen minutes a day.

4. Read the whole Bible in the order each event or writing took place. With this approach, you'll see the historical links between various parts of the Bible.

You can find each of these reading plans at biblegateway com/reading-plans/more. Enjoy!

*Lord, I thank You for the variety of ways I can
read Your Word. Which option should I choose?*

Friday

READ WITH GOD AT WORK INSIDE YOU

*I have hidden your word in my heart
that I might not sin against you.*
PSALM 119:11 NIV

When we read the Bible, we need to do so with our spiritual eyes wide open. How do we do that?

First, go to God in prayer. We can worship God, thank Him for His Word, and ask Him to remove anything that would cloud our hearts and minds as we read the Bible.

Next, ask God for the Holy Spirit's illumination as you read (and reread) each passage of scripture. We can read the same section of the Bible twenty, thirty, or forty times (or more) and still make new discoveries with each reading.

Finally, approach the Bible with a strong sense of expectancy, determination, and persistence. We need to look closely at scripture. The goal of such careful observation is to discover more and more of what God's Word says.

We're not conducting a superficial once-over, a cursory glance for some trivial tidbit. We're talking about looking intently at scripture and asking God to change us accordingly.

*Lord, I thank You for all the good You do inside
me when I read Your Word. I'm thrilled!*

Date: _____

Lord, You not only spoke the word to create the heavens and earth, but You also spoke the Word to some forty individuals who wrote down the inspired scripture. Thank You!

5 TOPICS COVERED THIS WEEK:

Monday: before you read the Bible
Tuesday: reading the Bible for the first time
Wednesday: how do I start reading the Bible?
Thursday: choosing a Bible reading plan
Friday: reading with God at work inside you

3 WAYS BIBLE READING LIFTS ME:

1. ....

2. ....

3. ....

3 WAYS BIBLE READING DEFLATES ME:

1. ....

2. ....

3. ....

How I want to respond to these truths:

....

....

....

....

....

....

....

....

....

....

LORD, HERE'S WHAT'S GOING ON IN MY LIFE RIGHT NOW. . .

OTHER THINGS I NEED TO
SHARE WITH YOU, LORD. . .

Lord, when it comes to this
new life map, I need to. . .

Open my eyes that I
may see wonderful
things in your law.
PSALM 119:18 NIV

Thank You, Lord, for
hearing my prayers
and for helping
me take action!
AMEN.

WEEK 6
Bible Study

Have you ever become painfully aware of a certain truth, but then chose to ignore (or conveniently forget) it?

We humans have an amazing capacity for knowing truth but going on our merry way as if we can somehow defy the odds, as if nature is obligated to make exceptions for us, as if reality will change to accommodate our forgetfulness or willfulness or stubbornness or arrogance.

It's amazing how, in this day of phenomenal technological advance and the explosion of knowledge, we humans can so easily ignore the obvious, the known, the true. It's as if common sense has been laid aside in favor of the latest fashions or fads.

Reality, however, has a way of slapping us in the face. No matter our age, education, social status, income, and net worth, reality allows no exceptions. And here is reality: God exists, created our world, and has certain expectations of us.

Of first importance, then, is our study of what the Lord says in His Word, the Bible.

> *"Keep this Book of the Law always on your lips; meditate on it day and night, so that you may be careful to do everything written in it. Then you will be prosperous and successful."*
>
> JOSHUA 1:8 NIV

Monday
TRUTHS TO AFFIRM

For the word of God is alive and active.
Sharper than any double-edged sword,
it penetrates even to dividing soul and
spirit, joints and marrow; it judges the
thoughts and attitudes of the heart.
HEBREWS 4:12 NIV

When you begin to read the Bible, it doesn't take long to discover it's full of literary genres. Within the thirty-nine books of the Hebrew scriptures (the Old Testament) and the twenty-seven Christian scriptures (the New Testament), you'll find historical accounts, poetry, laws, prophecy, and more. How do you make sense of it all?

Here's an approach: TA-CO, EH! It works from Mexico to Canada (everywhere, really). TA stands for "truths to affirm." CO stands for "commands to obey." And EH stands for "examples to heed."

As you read a section of scripture, simply ask yourself three questions. First, are there any truths to affirm? Second, are there any commands to obey? And third, are there any examples to heed?

The Bible is full of truths, but some have greater impact on our lives. The most important ones teach realities about the Lord God. The more we know and affirm them, the greater He will bless our lives.

Lord, I thank You for filling the Bible
with important truths. I believe them!

Tuesday
COMMANDS TO OBEY

*All Scripture is breathed out by God and profitable
for teaching, for reproof, for correction, and for
training in righteousness, that the man of God
may be complete, equipped for every good work.*
2 TIMOTHY 3:16–17 ESV

Yesterday I introduced the TA-CO, EH! Acronym. CO stands for "commands to obey." Would it surprise you to learn that the Bible isn't full of commands? A thousand-page Bible has, on average, only two commands per page, and nearly half are not applicable to you and me today.

While some commands take careful study to understand their intent and application, most are quite easy to understand—and should be obeyed.

Take what Paul says a minute later to Timothy: "Some people, eager for money, have wandered from the faith and pierced themselves with many griefs. But you, man of God, flee from all this" (1 Timothy 6:10–11 NIV). This injunction echoes what is taught by Moses and many others throughout scripture, including Jesus, multiple times. The verse speaks to our heart motives

Applicable to you and me? Yes!

*Lord, I thank You for Your commands, which provide
both a fence of protection and much freedom.*

Wednesday

EXAMPLES TO HEED

> For everything that was written in the past
> was written to teach us, so that through the
> endurance taught in the Scriptures and the
> encouragement they provide we might have hope.
> ROMANS 15:4 NIV

We're now at the end of the TA-CO, EH! Acronym. EH stands for "examples to heed." Some have asked why I don't say "examples to *follow*." That's because so many of the examples in the Old and New Testaments are negative.

Consider young David's amazing confession of faith in the Lord God, Creator of heaven and earth, right before fighting Goliath (1 Samuel 17:45–47). We can follow that example and daily praise and trust God. But then take the older David's decision to betray and murder one of his "mighty men," so he could take Uriah's wife. In doing so, David broke nearly half of the Ten Commandments. Not a path we want to take! If we "heed" this example, we'll go the other way every time.

The apostle Peter tells us to "follow in [Jesus'] steps" (1 Peter 2:21 NLT). How wonderful to remember Jesus was never hypocritical. He didn't just *say* walk a second mile, He did it. Jesus didn't just *say* turn the other cheek, He chose not to retaliate when He was slapped—hard. His is an example worth following!

*Lord, thank You for the positive and
negative examples in scripture. May I
gladly imitate and follow Jesus today.*

Thursday
APPLICATION VIA MEDITATION

His delight is in the law of the LORD,
and on his law he meditates day and night.
PSALM 1:2 ESV

Without application, the Bible makes no more difference in your life than water in a cooler, coffee behind the counter, or a fruit-flavored energy drink in a television commercial. There's no benefit unless you take it in.

That's why it's so important to meditate on scripture. It's not enough just to read words on the page. You and I need to wash our minds with God's Word. Meditation can involve:

- reflecting on the meaning of key words in a paragraph, verse, sentence, or phrase;

- memorizing a section of God's Word; or even

- rewriting a scripture passage in your own words.

James 1:25 (ESV) reminds us that "the one who looks into the perfect law, the law of liberty, and perseveres, being no hearer who forgets but a doer who acts, he will be blessed in his doing."

Throughout scripture God has promised to bless the woman who reads His Word, considers it intently, interprets it correctly then personalizes and applies it to her life.

Lord, please help me to read, reflect on, and
memorize scripture—then do what it says.

Friday

WRESTLING WITH UNANSWERED QUESTIONS

Your word is a lamp for my feet, a light on my path.
PSALM 119:105 NIV

As we read the Bible, we need to keep asking, "What did God mean by this statement?" As you go through scripture, write down your questions. Then seek answers.

If you don't have a study Bible, it's time to buy one. And your pastor or Bible study leader probably owns some commentaries you can borrow. But know that not all commentaries are created equal. If you're reading one (or any resource) that doesn't (1) worship God, (2) praise the Lord Jesus Christ, and (3) show tremendous respect for scripture, drop it fast and look for a better one!

Don't just Google your questions. There are reliable Bible software tools available, and your pastor would be a great resource on which ones to use. But ultimately, do your best to discover what God wants you to know. Most of the answers are right there in His Word.

In the end, it's okay to have some unanswered questions. I've held difficult passages in abeyance because no answer seemed satisfactory. Then a clear explanation will make it "fit" in my mind. Other questions will require a face-to-face with God in heaven. I can wait and trust Him for those answers!

Lord, thanks for welcoming tough questions.
Help me to dig deeply into Your Word for answers.

Date: ....

Lord, this week I learned not only what to look for when I read the Bible (TA-CO, EH!) but also how to go the second mile so Your Word makes a difference in my heart and mind.

5 TOPICS COVERED THIS WEEK:

Monday: truths to affirm
Tuesday: commands to obey
Wednesday: examples to heed
Thursday: application via meditation
Friday: wrestling with unanswered questions

3 WAYS BIBLE TRUTHS ANCHOR ME:

1. ....

2. ....

3. ....

3 WAYS BIBLE CHARACTERS CONFUSE ME:

1. ....

2. ....

3. ....

How I want to respond to these truths:

....

....

....

....

....

....

....

....

....

....

LORD, HERE'S WHAT'S GOING ON IN MY LIFE RIGHT NOW. . .

OTHER THINGS I NEED TO
SHARE WITH YOU, LORD. . .

Lord, when it comes to this
new life map, I need to. . .

Do not merely listen to
the word, and so deceive
yourselves. Do what it says.
JAMES 1:22 NIV

Thank You, Lord, for
hearing my prayers
and for helping
me take action!
AMEN.

55

WEEK 7
Church Attendance

Every man, woman, or child who follows Jesus Christ is a member of God's kingdom, God's family, and God's church. Jesus calls us to be active members of a local gathering of His followers: the hands-on expression of His church.

We sometimes forget the church is not just another human institution, but God's idea. Jesus founded it so His followers could more effectively make disciples through baptism, teaching His commandments, and remembering "I am with you always, to the very end of the age" (Matthew 28:20 NIV).

We live in Portland, Oregon, one of the least-churched cities in America, yet fourteen hundred churches here love Jesus and teach God's Word. You may live in a part of the country where attending church is expected, even if you aren't a believer. Maybe you've hardly ever attended church except on Christmas or Easter. Some have valid reasons for leaving a given church, but not for failing to join another. After all, we are blessed with plenty to choose from!

This week, discover how you can bless—and be blessed by—the church

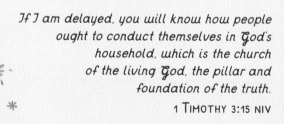

If I am delayed, you will know how people ought to conduct themselves in God's household, which is the church of the living God, the pillar and foundation of the truth.

1 TIMOTHY 3:15 NIV

Monday

VISIT ALL KINDS OF CHURCHES

In Christ we, though many, form one body,
and each member belongs to all the others.
ROMANS 12:5 NIV

In our family, moving to a new city has been a great opportunity to visit churches from A to Z. Attending different churches for a while may sound daunting, but when else do you have such a great opportunity to see the bigger church in action?

The reality is that every denomination has gifts for the rest of the church. What a joy to be blessed—directly or indirectly—by some of those gifts. Conversely, every denomination has a few customs or traditions that may feel peculiar to you. You may decide that you don't agree with them. In many cases, they're not wrong, just different.

Some denominations carry a rich sense of history. Some follow the church calendar and use liturgy, while others explore newer ways of worship. Some are small and provide close personal relationships. Some are large and offer great programs. Some support robust ministries locally, regionally, nationally, or overseas. Some proclaim the gospel and make an altar call every Sunday. Others emphasize deep discipleship.

The church is both God's family and Jesus' bride. The more you experience and love the whole church (starting with the people in your local church), the more you love Jesus Himself.

Lord, I thank You that I have so many opportunities
for seeing the bigger church in action.

Tuesday

NARROW YOUR OPTIONS

*Preach the word; be prepared in season and
out of season; correct, rebuke and encourage—
with great patience and careful instruction.*
2 TIMOTHY 4:2 NIV

After visiting a wide range of churches, it's important to decide which ones best fit you and your family. In our family, criteria include biblical preaching, music, ministries, theological compatibility, and open-handedness. The latter is a church's willingness to allow for differences on second- and third-level doctrinal matters. We have plenty of differences within our own family and relationships, and we want a church that allows for them.

We and our grown children attend a variety of denominations, yet we are all committed to the gospel of Jesus, scripture, and the "core" of orthodoxy (the primary truths taught and believed through the centuries). It's okay with my husband and me that our kids grew up and chose different churches.

In the end, selecting a church is both an objective issue (is it biblical?) and a subjective matter (is it a good fit?). Look at the church's schedule and programs. Consider the proximity of the facilities and other members. Get a feel for the values, style, and culture of the church. Above all, ask the Lord to guide you in this decision.

Then make a choice and settle in.

*Lord, I thank You for the freedom to attend and join
a church that both honors You and welcomes me.*

Wednesday

PLANT YOUR ROOTS DEEPLY

*Have confidence in your leaders and submit to
their authority, because they keep watch over
you as those who must give an account. Do this
so that their work will be a joy, not a burden,
for that would be of no benefit to you.*

HEBREWS 13:17 NIV

When our children grew up, they moved away to college, started careers, and chose new church homes. David and I have fellowshipped with the same church family for several decades. We didn't plan it that way, and we didn't always feel like staying— but we've reaped the blessings a thousand times over.

Once you've allowed for a trial period in a church, make a final decision and plant your roots deeply. Make a commitment to attend services every weekend. Join a small group for fellowship, prayer, and Bible study. Prayerfully join a ministry that serves in or through the church.

Committing to a local church means you'll experience the full scope of living together in community—the good, the bad, and the ugly. You'll share sorrows and joys and disappointment, whether in leaders, or fellow members, or even yourself. But in weathering the storms with your church family, you also will see God at work, creating beauty and fostering growth in each of your lives.

*Lord, I'm grateful that You created the church
as a place where I can grow and thrive.
Show me how to contribute to its success.*

Thursday

TWO VERY IMPORTANT INSIGHTS

*Then the church. . .enjoyed a time of peace and
was strengthened. Living in the fear of the Lord and
encouraged by the Holy Spirit, it increased in numbers.*
ACTS 9:31 NIV

David and I had the privilege of knowing Luis Palau, the renowned international evangelist. David worked with the Luis Palau Evangelistic Association for twenty years, and we enjoyed a personal friendship. Yet this man of God, committed to preaching the gospel around the world, planted his family's roots deeply into a local church.

Luis said, "By neglecting to minister within your local church, you cause other Christians to lose something. The Lord Jesus Himself says in John 15 that He is the vine, and we are connected to Him as branches. As a result, through Jesus, we are connected to each other. We are members of His body, the church."

Second, Luis added: "In 1 Corinthians 12:26 we read, 'If one part suffers, every part suffers with it; if one part is honored, every part rejoices with it.' How you relate or fail to relate to the body of Christ directly affects other Christians. We need each other!"

*Lord, You created the church to be a place
where You're tangibly at work. I'm thankful that
I can belong to Your family in a real way.*

Friday

THREE MORE INSIGHTS

*Let us consider how we may spur one another
on toward love and good deeds, not giving up
meeting together, as some are in the habit of
doing, but encouraging one another—and all
the more as you see the Day approaching.*
HEBREWS 10:24–25 NIV

David and I have never forgotten three more key principles Luis Palau taught us.

First, "When my family is ready to leave for church, we take certain expectations about what we want to get and leave them home with the dog." Go to church to give, not just receive.

Second, Luis added: "It is important to speak well of our church. Let your children hear you talking about our pastor, our elders, our Sunday school, our church retreat. This will help them claim the church as their own as they grow older." Address your concerns while preserving respect for your leaders and others.

Third, Luis made a point of saying that his particular church wasn't the biggest or best, and probably never would be. Be realistic in your expectations and lavish in your grace toward your church family.

We've lived these principles and found them to be solid.

*Lord, thank You for creating the church to
be a place where I can grow and thrive—
help me to bless and be blessed.*

Date: ....

Lord, You call me to be an active member of a local
expression of Your church. I want to discover how I
can bless—and be blessed by—that local body.

5 TOPICS COVERED THIS WEEK:

Monday: visit all kinds of churches
Tuesday: narrow your options
Wednesday: plant your roots deeply
Thursday: two very important insights
Friday: three more insights

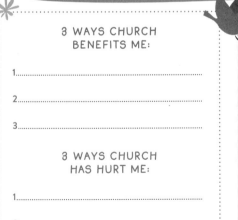

3 WAYS CHURCH BENEFITS ME:

1. ....

2. ....

3. ....

3 WAYS CHURCH HAS HURT ME:

1. ....

2. ....

3. ....

How I want to respond to these truths:

....

....

....

....

....

....

....

....

....

LORD, HERE'S WHAT'S GOING ON IN MY LIFE RIGHT NOW. . .

OTHER THINGS I NEED TO
SHARE WITH YOU, LORD. . .

Lord, when it comes to this
new life map, I need to. . .

You are a chosen people,
a royal priesthood,
a holy nation, God's
special possession, that
you may declare the
praises of him who called
you out of darkness into
his wonderful light.

1 PETER 2:9 NIV

Thank You, Lord, for
hearing my prayers
and for helping
me take action!
AMEN.

WEEK 8
Family, Part 1

Most young women plan to be married. Married women would say it's a rocky or wonderful experience—usually some of both. Marriage is two people coming together to become "one flesh" (Genesis 2:24). That takes teamwork. . .and it can be work.

For couples who share similar tastes, gifts, goals, and desires, teamwork is as smooth as pairs figure skating. They go through life hand-in-hand, moving together to the same music.

Other couples find their partnership is more like a track and field team. They're on the same team, but their lives are individual events. Though they're gifted and impassioned differently, they support and cheer each other on in their individual struggles and successes.

Sometimes a couple's marriage resembles a car race. The drivers are the stars of the show, but they wouldn't win anything without the pit crew's efforts at every stop. One of you may be up front, but you each contribute value.

Think about your interests and personalities. What kind of team would best represent you and your (possibly future) husband's relationship?

Over all these [Christian] virtues put on love, which binds them all together in perfect unity.

COLOSSIANS 3:14 NIV

AGREE ON SACRIFICES

Let no debt remain outstanding, except
the continuing debt to love one another,
for whoever loves others has fulfilled the law.
ROMANS 13:8 NIV

Similarities alone don't produce a good marriage partnership. What does? A strong commitment to each other's personal growth and a deep commitment to oneness before God. This week we'll look at five strategies my husband and I—and some of our closest friends—have used along the way.

The first strategy is most important: agree in advance on any sacrifices. Our friends Paul and Wendy have created a beautiful backyard sanctuary, but the years have not been a bed of roses! When Paul wanted to go back to school, it was a decision they made together. To prevent resentment, they consciously outlined what sacrifices they would (and wouldn't) make to realize Paul's goal of earning a doctorate in psychology.

They decided they could live with Wendy's almost full-time job out of their home and the need to live frugally. They would not accept drifting apart as a couple or shortchanging their time with their children. Paul and Wendy reached the other side with a strong marriage and family—and Wendy has learned a lot of counseling skills, too!

*Lord, what sacrifices would please You the
most? Please make them clear to both of us.*

Tuesday

DREAM TOGETHER

*Love never gives up, never loses
faith, [and] is always hopeful.*
1 CORINTHIANS 13:7 NLT

One marriage expert recommends that, on their anniversary each year, couples take one hour to dream together. He believes this will increase the longevity and happiness of a marriage. We agree!

Dreaming together deepens the spirit of partnership. Wherever the winds may blow us, we remember we are on the same ship. This kind of dreaming brought David and me to the place of adopting our youngest daughter, Anna. Now we're enjoying grandkids! Dreaming together has taken us to the Alps, the Andes, the Amazon, and Africa to visit beloved missionary friends.

Be willing to encourage and follow each other's dreams too. Who knows where your husband's next dream could take you? When David began dreaming about the two of us writing notes for the Living Faith Bible, I happily went along. In fact, I agreed to write three-fourths of the notes—and had the time of my life doing it. With this book project, we get to do it again!

*Lord, which of my dreams do You want me to
share with my husband? And which dreams do
you want me to lay aside, at least for now?*

Wednesday
CREATE A MISSION STATEMENT

*Let me hear of your unfailing love each
morning, for I am trusting you. Show me
where to walk, for I give myself to you.*
PSALM 143:8 NLT

A mission statement transforms dreams and desires into a tool you can grasp and use. Later, as needed, you can make revisions.

To create your mission statement, invite your husband to take some time away with you. This could be a weekend getaway or occur over the course of several dates. Categorize your individual gifts and passions in life. Make a list of your mutual desires and goals. Prioritize your time and talents—both as individuals and as a couple. Consider how you can use your differences to accomplish the mutual goals. Above all, pray for God to show you His desires. Ask Him to give you a mission by which to guide your marriage, both now and in the future.

Creating a mission statement helped our friends Troy and Shannon to thoughtfully say no to the constant moves that his career demanded. When he was diagnosed with cancer, their written purpose and priorities kept their marriage vision crystal-clear. When the disease claimed Troy's life, that mission statement was an incredible testimony to those who attended his memorial service.

*Lord, please help us to create a mission
statement that honors You.*

Thursday

DIVIDE AND CONQUER

*Let love and faithfulness never leave
you; bind them around your neck,
write them on the tablet of your heart.*
PROVERBS 3:3 NIV

Having similar gifts and callings is no guarantee that teamwork will flow naturally. When David and I were first married, he would take on classes for the two of us to teach "together." That translated into him giving me an outline or a script of what I should say. I balked because it felt artificial. It *was* artificial!

By the time we began working on the Living Faith Bible, however, we had learned to truly work together. We had a mutual goal but maintained our own autonomy. And still today, we divide the work and then each of us has full authority over our own portion of the project. When I write something, David can suggest specific things I might consider adding, deleting, or changing—but I always get the final say. For us, that feels like teamwork.

Many couples "divide and conquer" when it comes to the daily to-do of home and family. Ideally, you and your husband can focus on areas of personal strength and interest. When I went back to the university, David took over the laundry, but I kept cooking. That way, we were both happy!

*Lord, show us how to divide and conquer as a couple—
from our daily tasks to our largest goals and dreams.*

Friday

NURTURE YOUR TEAM SPIRIT

Above all, love each other deeply,
because love covers over a multitude of sins.
1 PETER 4:8 NIV

What should you do when "divide" leaves you feeling stuck with almost all of the work? And what about when "conquer" doesn't happen because you or your husband are overwhelmed by other stresses in life? That's when the spirit of "team" transcends the "work" in teamwork.

Sometimes all I need is God's reminder that we are, indeed, teammates—not opponents. Ultimately, David and I both want the same thing: to love God, to love each other, to love our children, to grow as people, to live in peace. Other times, when I have felt my team spirit waning, I pray more earnestly for David. Talking to God and asking Him to bless and help my husband realigns my heart with David's—and with God's.

Occasional selfish squabbles aside, David and I build our marriage partnership best when we heed God's calling. It's a calling to look not only to our own interests, but to the interests of others; to consider another as better than ourselves; and to lay down our lives for our very best, lifelong friend—our mate.

Lord, how can I best nurture and support my husband?
Guide me in Your way, and help me to act.

Date: ....

Lord, I thank You that family starts when You call a woman
and man to wed and then live together as "one flesh."
Thanks too for what I'm learning about marriage.

5 TOPICS COVERED THIS WEEK:

Monday: agree on sacrifices
Tuesday: dream together
Wednesday: create a mission statement
Thursday: divide and conquer
Friday: nurture your team spirit

3 WAYS MARRIAGE EMPOWERS ME:

1. ....
2. ....
3. ....

3 WAYS MARRIAGE BAFFLES ME:

1. ....
2. ....
3. ....

How I want to respond to these truths:

....
....
....
....
....
....
....
....
....

LORD, HERE'S WHAT'S GOING ON IN MY LIFE RIGHT NOW. . .

OTHER THINGS I NEED TO
SHARE WITH YOU, LORD. . .

Lord, when it comes to this
new life map, I need to. . .

So God created mankind
in his own image, in the
image of God he created
them; male and female
he created them.
GENESIS 1:27 NIV

*Thank You, Lord, for
hearing my prayers
and for helping
me take action!*
AMEN.

WEEK 9
Family, Part 2

God created Adam and Eve and called them to bring children into the world. Since then, each person finds his or her place in this experience called "family." Where do you find yourself in this continuum: granddaughter, daughter, sister, wife, aunt?

You can't escape the impact of the family you came from, but you can create beauty in a family, whatever your role. That's true whether or not you give birth, foster, or adopt children. Whether you live alone or with several generations, God can grow you through your family relationships.

Say "family," and for most people strong emotions arise. What kind of wisdom and planning can bring more joy and peace and growth to your family relationships? Let's explore that this week!

> *"Choose today whom you will serve. . . . As for me and my family, we will serve the LORD."*
>
> JOSHUA 24:15 NLT

Monday

HONOR YOUR PARENTS

*"Honor your father and mother"—which is
the first commandment with a promise—
"so that it may go well with you and that
you may enjoy long life on the earth."*
EPHESIANS 6:2–3 NIV

My parents saved my life. They trusted God and made choices to provide me with the safe, loving home they themselves hadn't experienced as children. My adopted daughter's parents destroyed her home—her good life now is the result of many years of love, commitment, and hard work.

You can't escape where you came from, but you can make new paths for yourself and your family. Begin by recognizing your identity in God's family. Do the work of acceptance and forgiveness.

If your parents are still living, your responsibility is to treat them as human beings made in the image of God—and loved by Him. Honoring them means acknowledging the gift of life they gave you. Ask God what He wants in your relationship with your parents, and then consider the following: What message can you tell yourself that honors your parents? What words can you say to your parents that will show them honor?

*Father, help me to show honor to the parents
who gave me life. May I extend the same
kind of love You have shown to me.*

Tuesday

BABY MAKES THREE

Children are a gift from the LORD;
they are a reward from him.
PSALM 127:3 NLT

Nothing changes things like a little person entering your world to stay. Your heart is full, your body is tired, and life is completely upended!

From the moment you first lock eyes, delight in her. Each time you respond to his cries and meet his needs, you build his ability to trust. Put down the phone, turn off the show, give your full attention. Remember she is a child—and only for a short while. He's immature because he's young. They're needy because they're small!

Books, podcasts, and classes can call give information on how to raise a child, but ultimately you will be the expert on this unique human being. You'll make mistakes, but you'll learn as you go. Take time, today and every day, to know your child as she grows. She needs both nurture and discipline that are specific to her.

And always, *always*, trust the Lord. Never forget that children are a gift, not a possession. God loves your kid(s) more than you possibly could. Yet He chose you to be this child's mother. And God makes no mistakes.

Lord, children are an incredible blessing—and challenge. Help me to love mine the way You love me!

Wednesday

THE LONGEST, FASTEST EIGHTEEN YEARS

These commandments that I give you today are to be on your heart. Impress them on your children.
DEUTERONOMY 6:6–7 NIV

When you're a parent, it seems like childhood will never end—until it does. Days are filled with getting the kids fed, clothed, and educated, driving them to a thousand play dates, practices, and games. How do you find the time to raise responsible, healthy, loving human beings?

Choose your family values and communicate them often—and live them out yourself. Live so that one day, your children say, "My mother always. . ."! They can't escape your words and habits.

Create good boundaries. Children need the safety of family rules and appropriate discipline. Your children need you to be the parent—they're not ready to be in charge.

But open doorways as they grow. Celebrate achievements. Give more responsibility and allow them to make more of their own choices each year. Children need to feel confident in their ability to "do life."

And build a village within your church family, neighborhood, or school district. Your child needs others to model, encourage, and fill in the gaps. Parenting isn't a solo journey!

Through it all, pray for your children. God molds their hearts.

Lord, strengthen me to guide my children that they may be the people we both want them to be.

Thursday

LOVING SOMEONE ELSE'S CHILD

*"Whoever welcomes one of these little
children in my name welcomes me."*
MARK 9:37 NIV

When I was a child, my parents fostered a child, welcomed in refugees from Vietnam, and adopted both my brother and two more sisters. My mother-in-law provided daycare and nurture for neighborhood children and drove countless more to church each week. Some homes are a hub for kids who need a place where they are listened to and loved.

God's heart beats strong for children. Jesus welcomed children with delight, and made it clear to His disciples that He expected them to do the same. Whether or not you're a "kid person," God wants you to welcome children too. Not just your own, but other people's.

What might happen if you said "yes" to God today? Start in the church nursery or teaching Sunday school, become a volunteer in your local school, take a niece or nephew to lunch or care for the baby so a young mom can have a break.

Or jump in deep—foster or adopt a waiting child. It takes making room in your home, your lifestyle, and your heart. But you'll be welcoming Jesus too.

*Lord, I want to welcome You. Show me how
to welcome a child who needs me.*

Friday

FRIENDS ARE FAMILY YOU CHOOSE

There is a friend who sticks closer than a brother.
PROVERBS 18:24 NIV

For most of history, a woman had few options outside her family. Unmarried women lived in their family homes for life—or lived by themselves in poverty or disgrace. Today, women enjoy incredible opportunities to create their own lives—along with the accompanying responsibilities.

In a world that's so big and yet so small, so connected and yet so isolating, a woman needs God, who never changes and who will never leave her. And a woman needs friends to love and be loved by.

I am blessed with a wonderful family of parents and siblings—but also select friends who have become family too. As I've grown and matured, I've learned what kind of people I need to be with and how I can give to others. I can accept people without needing them to be perfect or meet all my needs. I can enjoy what each friend has to offer and give my best to her.

Make the commitment to share life together with friends. Enjoy upbeat occasions in each other's homes. Be real and cry together in hard times. Pray for each other. Be loyal. Be family.

Lord, I need You, and I need other people.
Show me whom I can make a true friend.

Date: ....

Lord, I'm so glad You invented the family—
parents, children, even the friends we make in this
life. I will welcome and honor each one.

5 TOPICS COVERED THIS WEEK:

Monday: honor your parents
Tuesday: baby makes three
Wednesday: the longest, fastest eighteen years
Thursday: loving someone else's child
Friday: friends are family you choose

3 WAYS FAMILY BLESSES ME:

1. ....
2. ....
3. ....

3 WAYS FAMILY DRAINS ME:

1. ....
2. ....
3. ....

How I want to respond to these truths:

....
....
....
....
....
....
....
....
....

LORD, HERE'S WHAT'S GOING ON IN MY LIFE RIGHT NOW. . .

OTHER THINGS I NEED TO
SHARE WITH YOU, LORD. . .

Lord, when it comes to this
new life map, I need to. . .

Father of the fatherless
and protector of widows is
God in his holy habitation.
PSALM 68:5 ESV

*Thank You, Lord, for
hearing my prayers
and for helping
me take action!*
AMEN.

WEEK 10
Hospitality

How important is hospitality in your home?

Let's start with the people related to you. Many families have a hard time eating a single meal together each week, let alone every day. This despite extensive research showing the make-or-break factor in the average preteen's life is having at least five meals together with family each week. The meals don't need to be fancy—or even healthy! Just sitting down and eating together works the magic.

Down through the ages, in most cultures around the world, eating meals together has been the fabric of life. It's how life is lived within families, neighborhoods, and certainly in the biblical stories of the ancient Jewish people. The latter celebrated Sabbath meals, other religious get-togethers, and at least three multi-day national festivals each year.

Jesus and His apostles ate together often, as did the early believers who followed them. They also invited a wide assortment of other people to join them.

Hospitality was an expected part of each Christian's character and way of life. This week, let's make it a bigger part of your life too!

While Jesus was having dinner at Matthew's house, many tax collectors and sinners came and ate with him and his disciples.

MATTHEW 9:10 NIV

Monday
KEEP IT SIMPLE

*The Lord said to her, "My dear Martha, you are
worried and upset over all these details!"*
LUKE 10:41 NLT

Despite what the magazines imply, hospitality isn't about the food or décor—it's about making people feel welcome. Some women create amazing ambiance and meals, and I enjoy them thoroughly. But anyone can offer hospitality.

One friend came to my house and exclaimed, "Your house isn't perfect!" If that helped her feel more comfortable having people to her home, then I guess it's great. Clean the bathroom and change the cat box, but don't worry about having a perfect house.

And be flexible. One time, we wanted to have our pastor and his wife over for a meal, but he is allergic to cats. So instead of eating at our house, we picked up dishes at our favorite restaurant, made a green salad, and took it to them. The food and the company were great—location was incidental.

When Jesus was at Martha's house, He encouraged her to keep things simple. As much as Jesus enjoyed a good meal, fellowship with His friends was the true priority.

*Lord, please help me to focus on people, not on my
own image, when opening my home to others.*

Tuesday

HOST YOUR PASTOR FOR A MEAL

The jailer brought them into his house and set a meal
before them; he was filled with joy because he had
come to believe in God—he and his whole household.
ACTS 16:34 NIV

Church leaders are expected to show a high degree of hospitality, both in welcoming new members and actively caring for the regulars. In my church, the pastor and his wife are both introverts, but they invite people to their home regularly. One evening, among a small group of women, the wife spoke honestly yet without resentment about a struggle of hers: namely, doing the inviting but rarely being asked into other people's homes.

When David served as a lay pastor, we had people to our home often. Sometimes, he liked to invite himself over to visit other church members—especially when someone had moaned about never being visited by one of the pastors. "Don't I count?" he asked. They usually had to think about that one!

Who could you invite to your home in the coming weeks? Plan something simple, then make it a time to express care and appreciation.

Lord, I thank You for the pastors in my life.
Give me the courage to reach out to one of them today.

Wednesday

HOST A MISSIONARY FOR A MEAL

> When she and the members of her
> household were baptized, she invited us to
> her home. "If you consider me a believer
> in the Lord," she said, "come and stay at
> my house." And she persuaded us.
>
> ACTS 16:15 NIV

When I was growing up, my church emphasized missions. Every year, there was a large missions conference, and many of those in attendance came for a meal in our home. I heard their stories at the table and felt connected to the faraway people and places.

I wanted to give my children the same heart for the world, so David and I have often invited missionaries into our home. They were real people, not just a picture on the refrigerator. Our missionary friends shared their stories (even candy!) from their country, and also invested in our children's lives by getting to know them and praying for them.

Maybe you should get to know a missionary as a real person. Be interested in them as people, not just in the work they do. Above all, pray together before they leave. The strength and encouragement you receive will be double what you give!

Lord, I thank You for the missionaries my church supports. Remind me this week to find out who's coming home on furlough.

Thursday

INVITE THE UNINVITED

> *"But when you give a banquet, invite the
> poor, the crippled, the lame, the blind."*
> LUKE 14:13 NIV

Some people love meeting new people. . .but most of us prefer to stick to the friends we know, especially when it comes to sharing our time and homes. Jesus, though, bluntly told us to invite the uninvited. In the verse above, that means people whose income level or physical disability keep them out of regular social circles.

Remember that arranging for people with disabilities requires extra preparation. Offer transportation or meet in a restaurant if your home has stairs or narrow hallways.

You probably know people who struggle financially. Make sure to include them on the guest lists of your summer barbeques or holiday parties. Do whatever it takes to get over your own nervousness. Be unshockable when people reveal what they lack—and be ready with cash (not a check) to meet at least one specific need. The Lord promises to reward you.

Ask your church leaders for ideas, and they will be glad to help you know whom to bless.

> *Lord, I praise You for Your love of each
> person, no matter their status or ability.
> Please give me that same love.*

Friday

INVITE AN IMMIGRANT

*He defends the cause of the fatherless and
the widow, and loves the foreigner residing
among you, giving them food and clothing.*
DEUTERONOMY 10:18 NIV

David and I have been foreigners at scores of meals from the Amazon jungles to the Sahara Desert. We always enjoyed the generosity and good humor of our hosts, whether we had the meal of our lives or politely ate whatever was put before us.

Back home in the states, my parents went beyond just offering a meal. They hosted several Vietnamese refugee families in the 1970s and 80s. Today, refugee families from other countries still need host homes. How can you get to know immigrants personally? Contact a campus ministry group. International students come from all over the world to study in the United States, but rarely see the inside of an American home. In making an invitation, ask first about food preferences—no one expects you to know everything about their culture. And when they invite you to their home in return, say yes! More often than not, it will be the meal of your life.

*Lord, You've always had a great love for
foreigners. I thank You that so many want
an American friend. Make me one.*

Date: ....

Lord, I'm glad that hospitality is an expected part of each Christian's character and way of life. Please make it a bigger, more exciting part of my life in coming days.

5 TOPICS COVERED THIS WEEK:

Monday: keep it simple

Tuesday: host your pastor for a meal

Wednesday: host a missionary for a meal

Thursday: invite the uninvited

Friday: invite an immigrant

3 WAYS HOSPITALITY EXCITES ME:

1. ....

2. ....

3. ....

3 WAYS HOSPITALITY SCARES ME:

1. ....

2. ....

3. ....

How I want to respond to these truths:

....
....
....
....
....
....
....
....
....

LORD, HERE'S WHAT'S GOING ON IN MY LIFE RIGHT NOW. . .

OTHER THINGS I NEED TO
SHARE WITH YOU, LORD. . .

Lord, when it comes to this
new life map, I need to. . .

And do not forget to do
good and to share with
others, for with such
sacrifices God is pleased.
HEBREWS 13:16 NIV

Thank You, Lord, for
hearing my prayers
and for helping
me take action!
AMEN.

WEEK 11
Bible Memorization

The secret of memorizing anything is loving it. Whether it's sports statistics, music lyrics, or movie lines, people commit to memory what they think about most often. And what is fixed in our memory changes and shapes us.

Scripture memorization isn't a modern idea. For most of history, most individuals had no personal copy of the scriptures—if they could read at all. What they knew of the God's Word came from hearing it and committing it to memory.

I'm blessed that I began memorizing scripture as a child—not just the verses in my AWANA book, but whole chapters and verses for Bible quiz team competitions. In all honesty, after I turned twenty, I found that memorizing became more difficult. But having passages like Romans 8 in my mind and heart has impacted me and my relationship with the Lord profoundly over the years.

The secret to memorization is poring over something again and again, soaking it in and delighting in it. This week, I invite you to memorize five of the most famous and power-packed scripture passages. They will change you forever.

I will delight in your statutes; I will not forget your word.

PSALM 119:16 ESV

Monday

MEMORIZE DEUTERONOMY 10:12–13

> What does the LORD your God ask of you but to
> fear the LORD your God, to walk in obedience
> to him, to love him, to serve the LORD your God
> with all your heart and with all your soul, and to
> observe the LORD's commands and decrees that
> I am giving you today for your own good?
> DEUTERONOMY 10:12–13 NIV

Do you wonder what God wants most from you? Moses begins by asking this most vital question. Then he presents five very important answers:

1. "Fear the LORD your God."

2. "Walk in obedience to him."

3. "Love him."

4. "Serve the LORD your God with all your heart and with all your soul."

5. "Observe the LORD's commands and decrees that I am giving you today for your own good."

Each of these five very important answers reverberates throughout the rest of the Bible. So learn and love them well!

> *Lord, help me right now to memorize these verses.*
> *I thank You for calling me to say yes to You. I do!*

Tuesday
MEMORIZE PSALM 23:1–6

The LORD is my shepherd, I lack nothing. He makes
me lie down in green pastures, he leads me beside
quiet waters, he refreshes my soul. He guides me
along the right paths for his name's sake. Even
though I walk through the darkest valley, I will fear
no evil, for you are with me; your rod and your staff,
they comfort me. You prepare a table before me in
the presence of my enemies. You anoint my head
with oil; my cup overflows. Surely your goodness
and love will follow me all the days of my life,
and I will dwell in the house of the LORD forever.

PSALM 23:1–6 NIV

Tens of millions have memorized the most famous of the 150 psalms, and for good reason. It doesn't matter which Bible translation you use. . .Psalm 23 is always powerful.

In this psalm, David draws upon his years of experience as a shepherd to praise the Lord in picturesque, poignant, and poetic language. Specifically, David praises God for His (1) provision; (2) refreshment; (3) guidance; (4) protection and comfort; (5) anointing and joy; (6) goodness and love; (7) promise of heaven.

Could you use some of those realities today? Memorize this psalm and refer to it often.

*Lord, please help me to memorize Psalm
23 today. I praise You for Your many
benefits and blessings in my own life.*

Wednesday

MEMORIZE JOHN 3:16–18

For God so loved the world that he gave his one and
only Son, that whoever believes in him shall not
perish but have eternal life. For God did not send
his Son into the world to condemn the world, but
to save the world through him. Whoever believes in
him is not condemned, but whoever does not believe
stands condemned already because they have not
believed in the name of God's one and only Son.

JOHN 3:16–18 NIV

Countless millions of children have memorized the most popular Bible verse of all, John 3:16. What's not to love about this
winsome gospel sentence?

As adults, we would do well to memorize the apostle John's
next two verses as well. Verse 17 affirms God's intention: to
save us, not condemn us. Verse 18 confirms the two choices
before each of us: to believe in Jesus (who He is, what He did
for us) or not to believe (and stand condemned by the Judge
of all the earth).

That last part may sound harsh, and it is. But how good to
clearly know both choices before us. That way, no one need
worry or fret—which is in keeping with the Lord's heart of love.
He doesn't want anyone to perish. (If you want a very clear
statement of that, look at 2 Peter 3:9.)

Lord, I thank You for Your heart of love.
It is amazing—may I enjoy it and share it.

Thursday

MEMORIZE ROMANS 10:9–10

*If you openly declare that Jesus is Lord and believe
in your heart that God raised him from the dead,
you will be saved. For it is by believing in your
heart that you are made right with God, and it is by
openly declaring your faith that you are saved.*
ROMANS 10:9–10 NLT

We can't memorize too many gospel verses, and these two have been favorites of D. L. Moody, Billy Graham, Luis Palau, and other great evangelists—as well as hundreds of thousands of youth and children's workers. Both verses are simple enough for students to grasp and deep enough for theologians to ponder. These verses give us words to answer someone's question, "How do I become a Christian?"

Some translations use the words *confess* or *profess*, which are accurate, but the New Living Translation's phrasing of "openly declare" clearly conveys the apostle Paul's intent to today's readers. Here's an obvious question: In church, in small groups, in personal conversations, and on social media do we openly declare that Jesus is our Lord, Master, and King?

To be saved is to openly declare our trust in—and allegiance to—the Lord Jesus Christ, God's Son and our Savior. By memorizing this passage, you'll never forget that important fact!

*Lord, thank You for making the way so clear.
I'm so glad to openly declare my allegiance to You!*

Friday

MEMORIZE PHILIPPIANS 4:6–7

*Don't worry about anything; instead, pray
about everything. Tell God what you need, and
thank him for all he has done. Then you will
experience God's peace, which exceeds anything
we can understand. His peace will guard your
hearts and minds as you live in Christ Jesus.*
PHILIPPIANS 4:6–7 NLT

When you repeat these words to yourself, you'll savor them and come to know the rich sweetness of what they truly mean. When you're in the depth of a deep crisis, when you're so emotionally fried you can't read your Bible, these words will reach down into your soul. Nothing will calm your mind, relax your muscles, slow your heartbeat, and pace your breathing as quickly as the recitation of these two verses.

Don't miss the four plain commands in verse 6: (1) "Don't worry about anything"; (2) "pray about everything"; (3) "tell God what you need"; (4) "thank him for all he has done."

Obeying these commands defines much of what it means to "live in Christ Jesus" (end of verse 7). Actually doing what these verses say opens you up to experience God's unsurpassed, protective peace (the rest of verse 7). And by memorizing these verses, you'll be ready when worrisome situations arise.

*Lord, Your commands and promises are my comfort,
solace, encouragement, strength, joy, and peace.
Help me always to live according to Your Word.*

Date: ....

Lord, I'm so glad that the secret to memorizing anything
is delighting in it. As I memorize and review key verses of
scripture, increase my love for and delight in You.

5 TOPICS COVERED THIS WEEK:

Monday: memorizing Deuteronomy 10:12–13
Tuesday: memorizing Psalm 23:1–6
Wednesday: memorizing John 3:16–18
Thursday: memorizing Romans 10:9–10
Friday: memorizing Philippians 4:6–7

3 WAYS MEMORIZING SCRIPTURE DELIGHTS ME:

1...

2...

3...

3 WAYS MEMORIZATION FRUSTRATES ME:

1...

2...

3...

How I want to respond to these truths:

....
....
....
....
....
....
....
....
....

LORD, HERE'S WHAT'S GOING ON IN MY LIFE RIGHT NOW. . .

OTHER THINGS I NEED TO
SHARE WITH YOU, LORD. . .

Lord, when it comes to this
new life map, I need to. . .

"I am the vine; you are the
branches. If you remain in
me and I in you, you will
bear much fruit; apart from
me you can do nothing."
JOHN 15:5 NIV

*Thank You, Lord, for
hearing my prayers
and for helping
me take action!*
AMEN.

WEEK 12
God's Will, the General Issues

When we read Bible stories, it may feel like those people had easy access to God's voice and will. Actually, even the great saints of the Old Testament—Abraham, Sarah, Deborah, David, Daniel, and other prophets—only occasionally heard God's voice. A message from God or an angelic messenger came only a few times throughout their lives. The key factor when hearing from God was whether they obeyed.

You may wish that you knew God's will plainly—that He would speak to you in a dream or a sign so you could know which way to go. But God doesn't typically communicate His will or plans that way.

That's why it's so important to know and apply key biblical principles about the Lord's will. This week, we will explore five such principles rooted in scripture.

> *He has told you, O man, what is good; and what does the LORD require of you but to do justice, and to love kindness, and to walk humbly with your God?*
>
> MICAH 6:8 ESV

GOD'S WILL IS BIG

"This, then, is how you should pray: 'Our Father in
heaven, hallowed be your name, your kingdom come,
your will be done, on earth as it is in heaven.'"
MATTHEW 6:9–10 NIV

God's will is bigger than we could ever dream. Years ago, David
and I had such noble plans for me to finish college and then
for us to go to the mission field. We were committed to serving
God and eager to get where we wanted to go.

But God had different plans. He wanted to teach me that
He is more concerned with how we serve than where we serve,
with who we are than what we do.

A wise mentor told me, "Your life is like a pump in the
middle of a barnyard, isn't it? Anyone can get to you at any
time. The minute you see them coming, you know they want
something and they expect you to deliver. You feel handled,
don't you? Used. And that's good, isn't it? You want to be God's
servant, so of course everyone who walks by is going to pump
you. Your only problem is, your pipe isn't deep enough."

Lord, may my pipe go deep into Your nourishing
love. Fill up my reservoirs so that I am satisfied,
and then can pour out love to others.

Tuesday

GOD'S WILL IS MUNDANE

*"But seek first [God's] kingdom and his righteousness,
and all these things will be given to you as well."*
MATTHEW 6:33 NIV

God's will is more mundane than we would ever guess. Brother Lawrence, the seventeenth-century monk who wrote *The Practice of the Presence of God*, spoke of serving God while peeling potatoes. Around our house, two things reign supreme—dishes and laundry. Now that the children are gone, I prefer to leave the dishes to David. But laundry—I've always seen life there. Something about taking clean clothes from the basket and grouping them into logical piles does my heart good. A transformation from disorder to order—there's a promise and a sense of accomplishment.

Orderly piles of clean laundry give me a taste of what I'd relish in the rest of my life. Of course, the human beings who generate the content of those piles also help to create the hecticness that keeps my life spinning happily. So I enjoy my islands of order when I can, allowing them to spur me on to accomplish other mundane tasks.

To quote Brother Lawrence: "We ought not to be weary of doing little things for the love of God, who regards not the greatness of the work, but the love with which it is performed."

*Lord, You are in every task, no matter how
mundane. Therefore, I will do each one for You.*

Wednesday

GOD'S WILL IS HARD TO UNDERSTAND

*And we know that in all things God works for
the good of those who love him, who have
been called according to his purpose.*
ROMANS 8:28 NIV

God's will is harder to understand now than it is later. Someday, however, in the new heavens and new earth, I will have a glorified body, soul, and mind. And the intricacies of God's sovereignty coupled with human choices will, I believe, be displayed in such a way that we will stand back in awe and say, "So that's how it was done! Marvelous! Bravo!"

In the meantime, I have to accept my limitations. When it comes to many life topics, no problem. When it comes to advanced calculus and astrophysics, big problem. That doesn't mean the latter fall outside of God's perfect will. I just have to take their existence and applications by faith.

The Lord never answered Job's questions about why all those terrible things happened. What Job wasn't told then, we know now—but God's will in our own lives often remains a mystery. We can be sure, though, that He will work all things together for our good.

*Lord, how often I want to understand Your
will. But I also know You are growing my faith.
You are my Commander, Master, and King.*

Thursday

GOD'S WILL IS LESS EXCITING

*You need to persevere so that when you have done the
will of God, you will receive what he has promised.*
HEBREWS 10:36 NIV

God's will is sometimes less exciting than we might wish. Consider one man's story:

War had broken out, and the future of nations was at stake. Huge shipments of bullets arrived daily in a certain lab, where one specimen from each load was tested to ensure quality. The man in charge of the testing couldn't have been more qualified for the job—he was a true master. But a burning patriotism fueled the man's desire to be on the front lines of the war effort. Finally, he received his orders, said farewell to his staff (including one of my mentors), and went to the battle zone. And within a short time, he was gunned down by the enemy.

How tragic that this man couldn't see the tremendous significance of his behind-the-scenes contributions to the war effort!

Most of God's will is less than exciting. Of course, that's true of many of our responsibilities, on the job, at church, or in our home. But God doesn't call us to pursue what's thrilling. He calls us to persevere in doing His will.

Lord, help me to persevere in what You want me to do.

Friday

GOD'S WILL TAKES LONGER

*Now may the God of peace. . .equip you with
everything good for doing his will, and may he
work in us what is pleasing to him, through Jesus
Christ, to whom be glory for ever and ever. Amen.*

HEBREWS 13:20–21 NIV

God's will takes much longer than we expect. Sadly, most women fail to persevere in God's waiting rooms. Why? Here are several reasons:

First, most women keep their eyes on other people. Key question: "What difference would it make if I didn't care what everyone else thought?"

Second, most women keep their eyes on their own expectations. Two realities: My expectations determine my length of obedience; therefore, I need to embrace God's expectations. My own expectations may be frustrated, but my growth doesn't need to be stunted.

Third, most women keep their eyes on the problem. Unlike King Saul, his son Jonathan had simple confidence in the reality of the God he served, even when the situation seemed confusing (see 1 Samuel 14).

Fourth, most women rationalize that they know best when they get up and walk out of God's waiting rooms. Instead of giving up and doing life our way, let's look to the eternal prize.

*Lord, it's hard to wait—even at a stoplight.
From now on, I want to embrace waiting. Help me!*

Date: _____

Lord, I'm glad that You don't call me to pursue everything that's exciting and thrilling. Instead, You simply want me to persevere in doing Your will. That is my daily objective and goal.

5 TOPICS COVERED THIS WEEK:

Monday: God's will is big

Tuesday: God's will is mundane

Wednesday: God's will is hard to understand

Thursday: God's will is less exciting

Friday: God's will takes longer

3 WAYS GOD'S WILL REWARDS ME:

1. ....
2. ....
3. ....

3 WAYS GOD'S WILL ELUDES ME:

1. ....
2. ....
3. ....

How I want to respond to these truths:

....

....

....

....

....

....

....

....

....

....

LORD, HERE'S WHAT'S GOING ON IN MY LIFE RIGHT NOW. . .

OTHER THINGS I NEED TO
SHARE WITH YOU, LORD. . .

Lord, when it comes to this
new life map, I need to. . .

Moses did everything just as
the LORD commanded him.
EXODUS 40:16 NIV

Thank You, Lord, for
hearing my prayers
and for helping
me take action!
AMEN.

WEEK 13
God's Will, the Specific Issues

God's will isn't merely a set of general principles. At key points in life, His will becomes specific. This week, we'll consider five important personal issues: marriage, children, career, finances, and aspirations. The latter concerns what we really want to do in life.

Of course, what we want and what we get aren't always the same. Most women want to marry, but deeply struggle with the question, "Who should I marry?" Other women dream about launching into specific careers, only to see doors repeatedly close. Even when our heart's desire is to glorify God, we want to be certain we are making the right choices.

One of my mentors reminded me, "You'll always overestimate what you can do in a year and underestimate what you can do in five"—let alone in a lifetime. So let's be intentional about our life choices.

As in all of life, our focus needs to stay on the Lord God, Creator of heaven and earth, who knows the end from the beginning. . .and who walks with us each step of the way between now and glory.

> "Your [God the Father's] kingdom come, your will
> be done, on earth as it is in heaven."
>
> MATTHEW 6:10 NIV

Monday

GOD'S WILL: MARRIAGE

"If you do marry, you have not sinned."
1 CORINTHIANS 7:28 NIV

As a young girl and teen, I dreamed of being married and having a large family. But I didn't see myself as attractive, so I wasn't sure if that dream would ever come true. God's plan for me, however, included meeting David, learning to see myself as he sees me, and getting married partway through college. (So much for being single all my life!)

Many amazing young women would love to get married if they could meet the right man. I love being married, so I want that for them—but I believe that being single and making your own life is always better than a difficult marriage.

David and I encouraged our own children to become the right person before (and while) looking for the right person. Even more importantly, we strongly urged them to date and marry only people who loved the Lord deeply and were committed to lifelong personal growth and maturity. "After all," we said, "you can work through any marriage problems if you're both willing to grow."

Lord, thank You for marriage. Please show me
how to thrive in mine for years to come.

Tuesday
GOD'S WILL: CHILDREN

Children are a gift from the LORD;
they are a reward from him.
PSALM 127:3 NLT

As the eldest daughter in my family, I loved caring for my five younger siblings and dreamed of one day having a large family myself. Years later David and I agreed to have three children. He was concerned about my pregnancies and postpartum blues, so he willingly chose surgery to prevent any more. But we were open to adopting children if God directed.

Six years later I was mothering five children—our three and two foster daughters. Imagine our shock, then, to learn I was pregnant! Couples may plan, but God decides. We welcomed our second son with delight. Seven years later we adopted our youngest daughter. They were challenging, but so much fun.

When the kids became teenagers, parenting felt like wrestling alligators. We had to depend on God moment by moment. Our family and church family were our village, and we all made it through.

Children are a lot of work and expense, but they are always "a gift from the LORD. . .a reward from him." Whether you've had children or are hoping to, trust God to give you the family He has planned.

Lord, I need to trust You with everything,
but especially issues as large and
important as family. Guide me, I pray.

Wednesday
GOD'S WILL: CAREER

*Instead, you ought to say, "If it is the Lord's
will, we will live and do this or that."*
JAMES 4:15 NIV

As a mathematical genius, our oldest son had no interest in being a math teacher. Instead, he rocketed to the top of his university's software engineering program.

Imagine David's dismay, then, when our son told him he had just thrown away an amazing six-figure job offer from a leading tech company. David begged him to retrieve the letter and pray about it "at least overnight." Our son did, and is happily working for that tech giant today.

I dreamed of being a writer. As a girl, I hoped to write and publish children's novels. I haven't written any fiction yet, yet God has given me more publishing opportunities than I ever dreamed possible. I never pursued social work, but God moved my heart and then opened a door. I look back and see how He wisely prepared me for this career on the frontlines, working with foster children.

Whatever your education, skills, or training, just put them to use and let God direct your path The best career advice? Pray, work hard, and watch for the opportunities God unveils.

*Lord, I'm willing to pray and work
hard. Please guide and provide.*

Thursday

GOD'S WILL: FINANCES

"The LORD gave and the LORD has taken away;
may the name of the LORD be praised."
JOB 1:21 NIV

When we were first married, David and I were poor and unemployed. . .but happy. God provided a great job for David at the same time our money ran out. Twenty years later, his layoff prompted us to begin our own company. Between our home and business, our assets reached a nice, round figure, then doubled, then tripled. Our financial charts promised more of the same—or so we thought.

But without warning, our little company's largest clients pulled more than three hundred thousand dollars of work out from under us just as the national economy plummeted. Our asset pie chart flipped through the air and landed with a big *splat.* Our once-successful business failed, we went through bankruptcy and foreclosure, and David and I found ourselves once again as poor as church mice.

Is it wrong to have financial goals? No—but we need to hold everything with open hands. After losing his wealth, "Job did not sin by charging God with wrongdoing" (Job 1:22 NIV). In time, God doubly restored his fortune.

God hasn't doubled our fortune, but we have experienced His wonderful provision. We trust Him to provide for our needs, and pray and work toward the additional.

*Lord, I hold everything with open hands.
May Your name be praised.*

Friday

GOD'S WILL: ASPIRATIONS

Let God transform you into a new person by changing the way you think. Then you will learn to know God's will for you, which is good and pleasing and perfect.
ROMANS 12:2 NLT

Let's go beyond career and financial goals today. In the rest of life, what do you really want to do? "I don't know," you might be thinking "What else is there?" Here are several ideas:

First Tier
(1) Become a woman who loves God wholeheartedly. (2) Become a woman who loves others well. (3) Become a woman of good character. (4) Become a woman of goodwill in your community. (5) Become a leader in your church.

Second Tier
(6) Become a woman of good humor. (7) Become a woman who loves children well. (8) Become a woman who tells stories about her most embarrassing failures. (9) Become a woman who asks others, "What is your (life) story?" (10) Become a woman who invites others to church.

Third Tier
(11) Become a lifelong reader of good books. (12) Become a lifelong learner of God's wisdom.

Lord, I thank You for giving me so many opportunities to pursue. Show me who You want me to be.

Date: _____

Lord, my focus needs to stay on You for the rest of my life. After all, You know the end from the beginning, and You promise to walk with me each step of the way.

5 TOPICS COVERED THIS WEEK:

Monday: God's will: marriage
Tuesday: God's will: children
Wednesday: God's will: career
Thursday: God's will: finances
Friday: God's will: aspirations

3 WAYS GOD'S WILL IS CLEAR TO ME:

1. ....
2. ....
3. ....

3 WAYS GOD'S WILL IS A MYSTERY TO ME:

1. ....
2. ....
3. ....

How I want to respond to these truths:

....
....
....
....
....
....
....
....
....
....

LORD, HERE'S WHAT'S GOING ON IN MY LIFE RIGHT NOW. . .

OTHER THINGS I NEED TO
SHARE WITH YOU, LORD. . .

Lord, when it comes to this
new life map, I need to. . .

Who, then, are those who
fear the LORD? He will
instruct them in the ways
they should choose.
PSALM 25:12 NIV

Thank You, Lord, for
hearing my prayers
and for helping
me take action!
AMEN.

WEEK 14
Work, Part 1

This week, we're going to look at the world of work with some expert help from some friends of ours. Several are former Fortune 500 executives and consultants. Several others provide in-depth counseling to women (and men) at every career stage. They're quite a diverse group with some great things to teach us.

Some people bristle at the idea that anyone else has something to teach them. But when we think that way, we're choosing the pathway of mediocrity and eventual failure. Why would anyone do such a thing? The answer is easy: stubborn pride.

The wise woman seeks to grow in the Lord and in every major sphere of life—including her work. After all, work is where we invest many of our waking hours each week. Want to be successful? Then learn from the best.

This week, ask God to help you learn five key insights for success!

> *By the grace of God I am what I am, and his grace to me was not without effect. No, I worked harder than all of them—yet not I, but the grace of God that was with me.*
> 1 CORINTHIANS 15:10 NIV

Monday

STRENGTH AND DEPENDENCE

"There are many virtuous and capable women
in the world, but you surpass them all!"
PROVERBS 31:29 NLT

I did it the hard way, but I finally learned I have two kinds of strengths.

Natural strengths are certain traits of personality that God gave me. If I operate within these strengths, I thrive. Conversely, if I try to convert a personal weakness into a strength, and then seek to operate out of this "learned" strength, I may thrive for a time—but then I crash. Why? Because it takes so much work to operate out of learned strengths, I either burn out or flee back to my natural strengths. Either way, what looked like a great start can become a huge mess.

One of my big goals is to operate out of my natural strengths, empowered by God, so I can thrive. May you thrive too! Toward that end, I recommend that you read *Grace Revealed: Finding God's Strength in Any Crisis*. It's written by our good friend Fred Sievert, former president of New York Life Insurance. He's more successful—and dependent on God—than most anyone else.

Lord, help me to know what strengths You gave
me, and use them in dependence on You.

Tuesday

DISQUIET AND DELIVERANCE

Why are you cast down, O my soul? And why are you
disquieted within me? Hope in God; for I shall yet
praise Him, the help of my countenance and my God.
PSALM 42:11 NKJV

A dedicated, successful, and hardworking leader told David about some serious problems within his organization. David replied: "Is it possible that your personal issues have colored or clouded your perceptions?" In this case, the answer, sadly, was a clear "yes."

A book David highly recommended that this man read is The Disquieted Soul. It's written by a good friend, Lane Cohee, a former executive in the defense and aerospace sector.

"For as long as I can remember," Lane writes, "I have lived with a decidedly disquieted soul—a soul perpetually fueled by flames of anxiety and discontent. Over the years I rarely gave it serious thought, assuming that there were many more important matters in life. There are not."

Lane adds: "In my experience, nothing is more important to recognize and remedy because, left unchecked, a disquieted soul is spiritually suicidal by nature. It ultimately charts a path of its own undoing" (emphasis his).

How is your soul at home? At work? At rest? In times of disquiet, what is the psalm writer's remedy?

Lord, I feel disquieted right now.
Change my perceptions. Turn my gaze
toward You. Be my joy and peace.

Wednesday

QUESTIONS AND WISDOM

*When the queen of Sheba heard about the fame
of Solomon and his relationship to the LORD,
she came to test Solomon with hard questions.*

1 KINGS 10:1 NIV

Each day this week I'm recommending a great book from the world of work. Today's is an e-book, *Leading with Questions*. It's written by Bob Tiede, who has trained untold thousands how to ask the right questions and pursue the right answers.

Bob writes: "Jesus did two things exceedingly well: He told great stories and He asked great questions " Of course, Jesus' stories always provoked questions, so He must have *loved* questions!

Like Bob, David and I have thought a lot about Jesus and questions. Like you, we've heard people ask, "Is Jesus Lord of your life?" He is, now and for eternity. The better question is, "Have you acknowledged that fact?" How good it is to gladly acknowledge the Lord's place in the universe—and in your life and mine—here and now.

How does this apply to your work? If the entire universe was created through Jesus (Colossians 1:16), then He certainly knows your best fit in a job and career. Be sure to ask Him about it.

*Jesus, I gladly acknowledge You as Lord of my
life. Any other response is unworthy of You and
unfitting for the woman You've made me to be.*

Thursday

LOVE FOR GOD, OTHERS, SELF

"The second is this: 'Love your neighbor as yourself.'
There is no commandment greater than these."

MARK 12:31 NIV

I've learned that every Christian needs to ask three probing questions. I only wish I had known these questions a few years ago:

1. Do I understand the greatest commandment and take it seriously?

2. Do I understand that I can love God wholeheartedly only if I have received, embraced, and cherished His deep love for me?

3. Do I understand that I can love my neighbors as myself only if I love myself?

If you're missing that final point, then the greatest commandment is mere theory. Granted, you may be working hard. Your work may astound others. But let's not kid ourselves—you're not fully engaged, with others or yourself.

To become fully engaged, I recommend you read *The Missing Commandment: Love Yourself* by our good friends Jerry and Denise Basel, who lead a counseling ministry north of Atlanta. Their teaching resolved a deep, nagging question in my own life: What does it mean for me to obey Jesus and love others "as yourself"? It may help you just as much as it helped me.

*Lord, thank You for speaking to my
own heart. May I listen intently.*

Friday

ANGER AND TRUE REPENTANCE

> But now you must also rid yourselves of all
> such things as these: anger, rage, malice,
> slander, and filthy language from your lips.
> COLOSSIANS 3:8 NIV

If there's anything worse than uncontrolled anger in the workplace, it's uncontrolled anger at home. If you struggle with anger, I recommend *Confessions of an Angry Man*. It's written by our good friend Brent Hofer.

Brent writes: "Despite the truth that I had driven my wife to reject me, I knew a more important truth: God loved me. And He had the ability to transform the world that I had ruined. The gospel was true, after all!

"I came to believe that God was working for my good. He didn't want me angry and dominating my wife and children. He wanted me changed and He had not given up on me. My life was not over and I was not alone in the dark."

Brent found that his wife would be the key God used to unlock the shackles of his anger. God often uses the people closest to us—our family, our friends, our coworkers—to get our attention, as long as we're willing to listen. Has anyone been trying to get a message through to you lately?

> *Lord, give me ears to listen—to Your Word,
> and to the loving people You've put in my life.*

Date: _____

Lord, the wise woman seeks to grow in You and in every major sphere of life—including work. After all, work is where many of us invest substantial waking hours each week.

5 TOPICS COVERED THIS WEEK:

Monday: strength and dependence
Tuesday: disquiet and deliverance
Wednesday: questions and wisdom
Thursday: love for God, others, self
Friday: anger and true repentance

3 WAYS LEARNING FROM OTHERS EMPOWERS ME:

1. ....
2. ....
3. ....

3 WAYS LEARNING FROM OTHERS FRUSTRATES ME:

1. ....
2. ....
3. ....

How I want to respond to these truths:

....
....
....
....
....
....
....
....
....

LORD, HERE'S WHAT'S GOING ON IN MY LIFE RIGHT NOW. . .

OTHER THINGS I NEED TO
SHARE WITH YOU, LORD. . .

Lord, when it comes to this
new life map, I need to. . .

Whatever you have
learned or received or
heard from me, or seen in
me—put it into practice.
PHILIPPIANS 4:9 NIV

Thank You, Lord, for
hearing my prayers
and for helping
me take action!
AMEN.

119

WEEK 15
Work, Part 2

This week, ask God to help you learn five more key insights for success in the workplace. We have expert help again from some Fortune 500 executives and consultants. Others are experts in the worlds of sports memorabilia, biblical tourism, and investment and entrepreneurship. Again, it's quite a diverse group with some great things to teach us!

But even better than what they know and have done, these men exemplify life mapping at its best. This week we'll learn how to recognize your worth at work, and then find work that's a joy, work that feels like home, work that challenges, and work that wins both now and in the future.

If you were to have coffee with our first expert and his wife, they would be quick to say it's never too late to life-map the rest of your career. But don't emphasize where you're going to work—focus on the kind of woman you're going to be.

My son, do not forget my teaching, but let your heart keep my commandments, for length of days and years of life and peace they will add to you. Let not steadfast love and faithfulness forsake you; bind them around your neck; write them on the tablet of your heart. So you will find favor and good success in the sight of God and man.

PROVERBS 3:1–4 ESV

Monday

RECOGNIZE YOUR WORTH AT WORK

> May the Lord our God show us his approval
> and make our efforts successful.
> Yes, make our efforts successful!
> PSALM 90:17 NLT

Success is a funny word. It can indicate doing whatever it takes to climb your way to the top. It can also mean recognizing your worth at work based on what God says about who you are and what you're supposed to do. "Once you understand the why behind work, you'll be able to pursue your career with confidence, embrace change, and approach your job with a whole heart—one that is fully submitted to God and ready for what He's called you to do. That's what makes work worth doing."

That's a quote from my good friend Tom Heetderks and his excellent book, *Work Worth Doing*. I especially love his seven Smart-with-Heart Actions, which emphasize the key verse 1 Samuel 16:7: "The LORD does not look at the things people look at. People look at the outward appearance, but the LORD looks at the heart" (NIV).

Imagine God filling both your heart and smiling as you work. It's possible every day!

Lord, I thank You for making Your home in me,
for working in me. Please help me to feel Your
approval and recognize my God-given worth on the job.

Tuesday
WORK THAT'S A JOY

Whatever your hand finds to do,
do it with all your might.
ECCLESIASTES 9:10 NIV

When we were kids, everyone asked, "What are you going to do when you grow up?" Interestingly, experts now say what we loved to do as girls is usually one of the top three indicators of our best career choices.

I read voraciously as a child, getting lost in good novels. I've also kept journals off and on since I was eight years old. Though I haven't mastered the crafting of a novel plot, I can tell a great story. And I've done that for love (not money!) at camps and retreats.

One book I loved in my childhood starred a nurse who helped families in the inner city. I gobbled up that biography of Jane Addams, cofounder of Hull House, the famous settlement home in Chicago. I never consciously thought of being a social worker, but I followed God's leading—and He brought me to a place where I do the very work I read about as a girl. Plus, I write!

What did you love doing as a kid? What might that indicate about work you could enjoy?

*Lord, I want my work to align with the skills
and passions You've given me. Please help me
to find wise counsel and work that's a joy.*

Wednesday

WORK THAT FEELS LIKE HOME

*Jesus said, "Come to me, all of you who are weary
and carry heavy burdens, and I will give you rest."*
MATTHEW 11:28 NLT

Andre Moubarak was born into a Christian family that lived along the Via Dolorosa in Old Jerusalem's Christian Quarter. He begins his book *One Friday in Jerusalem* by describing how he played on the Way of Sorrow's ancient stones. Its winding pathway and sites "are as familiar to me as your living room is to you." Today Andre is an ordained minister and licensed tour guide who helps people see the Bible anew through Middle Eastern eyes.

Many girls move away for college, then move again for their first career job, and never return to their childhood roots. Andre was able to find work that feels like home. Does any part of his story resonate with you?

Are you sometimes wistful for new and exciting opportunities? Ask God to open doors, and don't overlook the opportunities that your family roots might offer as you pursue meaningful work.

*Lord, You know what's best for me and my
family. Please guide me into the place that
brings You glory—and me contentment.*

Thursday

WORK THAT CHALLENGES

Do you see someone skilled in their work?
They will serve before kings; they will not
serve before officials of low rank.
PROVERBS 22:29 NIV

If you know you're going to live forever, what risks are you willing to take here on earth?

As a young man, my husband pulled off several life-threatening stunts, including glissading. None of those things were motivated by God, though. It's only by His grace that David lived long enough to marry me! Our good friend Curt Laird, however, was attracted to his future wife precisely because she (like he) is absolutely fearless.

Curt has worked in more than thirty countries. Among many achievements, he built successful businesses across war-torn Afghanistan—including a billion-dollar mobile phone company. In his book *The Culture Key*, Curt unpacks the underlying principles that govern business in these geographies. I especially like his Belief Tool, which has many applications for those of us who live and work in the United States.

Your boss may never ask you to work overseas though she could. Or what if your boss offered you a leadership training program? Or some other challenge that stretched you? Would you be willing to say yes? If so, God may use you in ways you never dreamed possible.

Lord, I'm willing to following Your leading anywhere.

Friday

WORK THAT WINS

"In the same way, let your light shine before others, that they may see your good deeds and glorify your Father in heaven."

MATTHEW 5:16 NIV

Will your job even exist in five or ten years? My husband's good friends Mitch Little and Hendre Coetzee doubt it. In their book *Shiftability*, they write: "We could almost say anyone in any business role today faces an uncertain future. We live in an age of disruption and disintermediation. The business landscape is rapidly and radically changing and it keeps getting harder to predict what lies ahead."

So what do you predict about your own job? Will it look the same in a few years? Will it be there at all? Or should you be making shifts to your work mindset now? In other words, what limiting beliefs should you shed in order to successfully prepare for your future work?

Mitch and Hendre are both enthusiastic about the opportunities ahead. Keep that in mind as you fill out this weekend's Life Map. God has great plans for you.

Lord, I want to be open to changing how I think so that I'm ready for whatever happens to my work. Guide my career, I pray!

Date: _____

Lord, I want to recognize my worth at work based on what
You say about who I am and what I'm supposed to do.
Please fill my heart with Your wisdom and smile over my work.

5 TOPICS COVERED THIS WEEK:

Monday: recognize your worth at work

Tuesday: work that's a joy

Wednesday: work that feels like home

Thursday: work that takes courage

Friday: work that wins

3 WAYS THAT WORK BUILDS ME UP:

1. ....

2. ....

3. ....

3 WAYS THAT WORK GRINDS ME DOWN:

1. ....

2. ....

3. ....

How I want to respond to these truths:

....

....

....

....

....

....

....

....

....

....

LORD, HERE'S WHAT'S GOING ON IN MY LIFE RIGHT NOW. . .

OTHER THINGS I NEED TO
SHARE WITH YOU, LORD. . .

Lord, when it comes to this
new life map, I need to. . .

For God has not given
us a spirit of fear and
timidity, but of power,
love, and self-discipline.
2 TIMOTHY 1:7 NLT

*Thank You, Lord, for
hearing my prayers
and for helping
me take action!*
AMEN.

WEEK 16

Rest

After God spoke the universe into being, He wasn't winded. In creating Adam and Eve and planting a garden for them, God didn't break a sweat. Yet the Bible says, He "rested" (Genesis 2:2). God's rest was a quiet period of satisfaction and completion, not exhaustion. If He rested, how much more vital is it for His creatures to rest!

Later, God gave the Israelite people a day of rest: the Sabbath. While we no longer live under the law of Moses, our need for rest remains the same.

Jesus, who is fully God, was also fully man when He walked this earth. He grew tired and needed to sleep. He got weary and needed to refresh His body and soul. How can we follow His example?

Rest isn't primarily about sitting still. Rest happens throughout the day when we pace our minds and emotions, when we intentionally live within the limits of our bodies, and when we purposefully care for our souls.

> *"In returning and rest you shall be saved;*
> *in quietness and in trust shall be your strength."*
> ISAIAH 30:15 ESV

Monday
REST YOUR MIND

You [the LORD] will keep in perfect peace those whose
minds are steadfast, because they trust in you.
ISAIAH 26:3 NIV

In our current age, our minds can be both woefully stunted and overly stimulated. Screens flash images and pour out alarming information every moment, night and day. Resting our minds is more vital than ever.

Our brains weren't designed for nonstop stimulation. Even small choices suck our mental energy. I refuse to waste time picking out the "right" toothpaste or cereal. Save your brainpower for the big decisions!

When my mind races at night or wanders during the day, I stop and write myself a note—either on paper or via text or email. It's just a reminder to deal with a particular task or problem later. I know the message is waiting for me and I will come back and get it later, but I don't need to think about it when I should be sleeping or doing another task.

Mental focus isn't easy, but it is possible—and it provides rewards. When you specifically recall the good gifts God gives you, you're exhibiting trust in Him. The peace He gives will grow as your mind is preoccupied with thanksgiving.

Lord, so many thoughts bombard my brain.
I want to rest my mind on You.

Tuesday
REST YOUR EMOTIONS

[Jesus said,] "Come to me, all you who are weary
and burdened, and I will give you rest."
MATTHEW 11:28 NIV

I'm known for saying, "I need to save my emotional energy!" I also say, "It takes a lot of effort to save my energy!" My emotions can run like a stampede of wild horses.

Our emotions matter. We need to learn from them and use them to enrich our lives. A good cry can rest our emotions. So can a good laugh. But our emotions, especially certain types, can drive us over the cliff if we let them.

For example, guilt. Guilt tells us something is wrong. The correct response is to seek forgiveness and repair the wrong if possible. But feeling guilty all the time wears you out and doesn't do any good. Remember, Jesus takes your guilt away!

I'm also thinking of fear, which is the opposite of trust. Trusting God calms our minds and emotions. We face many hard, frightening things in this life, but Jesus promises to give us rest.

To rest your emotions, focus on just how much God loves and cares for you. Nothing else will help like He can.

Lord, I want to find rest in my emotions.
Please help me to trust You.

Wednesday

ENJOY GOOD NIGHTS OF SLEEP

*I lie down and sleep; I wake again,
because the LORD sustains me.*
PSALM 3:5 NIV

I struggled with insomnia for many years. I could go to sleep quickly, but I woke up later with my mind racing. And I would lie there for a long time before sleep returned.

Finally, I learned to embrace my waking time in those early, dark hours. So now when I find myself awake, I get up, make myself a cup of tea (maybe even some toast), settle on the couch with my Bible and some soothing music, and enjoy a quiet time with God. I spend the hour with Him instead of tossing and turning in bed. Before long, I'm ready to fall back asleep again before I need to get up for the day.

Going to bed at the same time every night helps our sleep. And so does keeping the bedroom's temperature a few degrees cooler than normal. Turn off all screens at least an hour before retiring, and make sure the television is in another room.

God made the human body to need rest. Don't short-circuit that good night's sleep He offers.

*Lord, show me what I can do to
enjoy good nights of sleep.*

Thursday

PROTECT YOUR MORNINGS

In vain you rise early and stay up late, toiling for food to eat—for [the LORD] grants sleep to those he loves.
PSALM 127:2 NIV

No, I'm not telling you to get up at five a.m. for your quiet time. If you can, that's wonderful, but "protecting your morning" means starting off your day from a place of peace and rest rather than franticness. I like to get up half an hour earlier than I need to, just so I can start off slow, sitting on the couch with a cup of coffee.

I learned the "protect your mornings" phrase at a workshop about living with second-hand trauma. It certainly applies to a close friend who is living through a time of ongoing rejection from an adult child and the demands of caring for elderly parents. After my friend's mother-in-law passed away, she and her husband decided to make a major change: to start their mornings slowly instead of rushing into each day's demands. Wise choice!

What might you change to protect your mornings? Is there anything in the previous evening that could go, to allow you to start the next day strong?

Lord, show me what I can do to protect my mornings.

Friday

SCHEDULE YOUR SABBATHS

He [Moses] told them, "This is what the LORD
commanded: Tomorrow will be a day of complete
rest, a holy Sabbath day set apart for the LORD."
EXODUS 16:23 NLT

A Sabbath is a time dedicated to doing something different from other periods of time. In the Bible, the Sabbath meant a day without work each week—each Sabbath started early Friday evening and finished early Saturday evening. They were days of rest and worship and reflection, days typically spent in one's home or courtyard with a break to attend the synagogue.

In our busy lives, Sabbaths are more important than ever. We need to practice resting on an intentional, regular basis. Even if you can't start with a whole day, try it for a morning or afternoon. Schedule your Sabbaths on Sundays, or Saturdays, or another day of the week if your work schedule demands.

Don't do chores on the Sabbath. Instead, prioritize rest and reflection. Include Bible reading, prayer, praise, and other forms of worship. Enjoy a good meal and time with people you love. Make your Sabbath rest a time of happiness and refreshment rather than duty, and you will be fully rested indeed!

Lord, which day should I choose for a Sabbath?
What do You want me to do—and not do?

Date:

Lord, help me to slow down when I'm tempted to work too hard,
too long, and for too many ultimately unimportant reasons.

5 TOPICS COVERED THIS WEEK:

Monday: rest your mind
Tuesday: rest your emotions
Wednesday: enjoy good nights of sleep
Thursday: protect your mornings
Friday: schedule your Sabbaths

3 WAYS REST HELPS ME:

1.
2.
3.

3 WAYS REST CONCERNS ME:

1.
2.
3.

How I want to respond to these truths:

LORD, HERE'S WHAT'S GOING ON IN MY LIFE RIGHT NOW. . .

OTHER THINGS I NEED TO
SHARE WITH YOU, LORD. . .

Lord, when it comes to this
new life map, I need to. . .

May the God of hope fill
you with all joy and peace
in believing, so that by the
power of the Holy Spirit
you may abound in hope.

ROMANS 15:13 ESV

Thank You, Lord, for
hearing my prayers
and for helping
me take action!
AMEN.

WEEK 17

Recreation

God created humans to explore and discover and enjoy the world He made. But as finite beings, we can't just keep going. Just as we need rest, we also need restoration.

Recreational activities engage our minds and bodies in new ways, providing much-needed enjoyment. Recreation can happen anywhere, but getting outside in our very "inside" culture enables our minds and bodies to renew. Not surprisingly, practitioners of both physical and mental health recommend time in nature on a regular basis.

My employer sends a monthly email encouraging "wonder walks" in nature to cultivate awe, the heightened awareness of beauty and mystery. How easy to walk in wonder when you already know the Creator and can fully enjoy all He has made.

This week, let's look at recreation in a new way—not just as another activity, but as a practice of refreshment. Let's explore how to re-create our mind, body, emotions, and spirit.

> *There is a time for everything, and a season for every activity under the heavens.*
> ECCLESIASTES 3:1 NIV

Monday

RE-CREATE OUTDOORS

*O LORD, what a variety of things you have
made! In wisdom you have made them all.*
PSALM 104:24 NLT

My friend Julie went with her family up to the mountain to ride inner tubes. After a slow start (you have to buy tickets and use the bathroom, you know), they finally found the youth group whose activity they were joining. Julie's family was over-dressed and soon sweating.

The hassles could have stressed out Julie, but she found herself happy and invigorated. Not just by the fresh air, but by visiting a unique and beautiful place as a family. She wondered, "Why haven't we done this before?"

As I write this devotional, I'm looking out over the Pacific Ocean. I come to the picturesque Oregon coast at least three times a year and I always feel renewed by it. Sometimes David and I bring friends and enjoy games of bocce. We always enjoy long walks on the beach.

Now I'm wondering: how will I re-create the rest of the year? We'll consider that question together this week.

*Lord, I thank You for the variety of
ways we can re-create outdoors.*

Tuesday

PLAN AHEAD SO YOU CAN PLAY

[Jesus] said to them, "Come with me by
yourselves to a quiet place and get some rest."
MARK 6:31 NIV

Open your calendar today and schedule some days for recreation, even if you don't know what activities you'll do. If you don't set time aside for recreation, the days will fill up with other things. Planning ahead helps to ensure recreation happens—and provides opportunity for more time with the key people in your life.

Need ideas? Look up events in your community and consult your local parks and recreation website. Peruse the brochures at a nearby hotel for excursions and tours. Nature societies offer specialized hikes and learning experiences. Pretend you're a tourist and explore your own community! Take a day trip by car, bus, or train to a different city—or drive through the countryside stopping at local fruit stands.

You can even ask your friends to include you in their recreational activities. When you're looking to improve your mental and emotional health, why not include the important people God's put into your life?

*Lord, please help me to plan for recreation. I know
I'll be happier and better able to represent You.*

Wednesday

FIND YOUR BEST FIT

*Every skilled woman spun with her
hands and brought what she had spun—
blue, purple or scarlet yarn or fine linen.*
EXODUS 35:25 NIV

Not every activity refreshes your body, soul, and spirit. Trying new things enriches you, but doing what you *love* rejuvenates you. What are your recovery needs? Something that slows your mind and body—or something that gets your heart rate pumping? What about activities that allow you to lose track of time and let your creativity flow?

My friends Brenda, Liz, and Paulette create order and beauty through their sewing. Sewing stresses me—but I love picking berries and making jam. Other women bike, swim, paint, or craft. Our friends Jodie and Troy use wheelchairs and no longer drive, but they take the metro to attend street fairs, festivals, and outdoor concerts.

I find refreshment strolling through the wooded park near our home. When I fill my lungs with forest-scented air, my shoulders relax and my eyes are drawn up to the trees and the sky. My mind settles down and my spirit praises God.

What's your best fit? How might it refresh your spirit and point you to God?

*Lord, I thank You that You're always ready to bless
me physically, mentally, emotionally, and spiritually.*

Thursday
PAY FOR YOUR PLAY

Whatever is good and perfect is a gift coming
down to us from God our Father, who created
all the lights in the heavens. He never
changes or casts a shifting shadow.
JAMES 1:17 NLT

Budget for and invest in recreation. You might join a local rec team for a reasonable fee or get a pass to the nearest public swimming pool, YMCA, or state or national park.

My son-in-law grew up skiing, but that wasn't something we did with our kids. My daughter, though, eventually took a college elective to learn—and got engaged on a black diamond slope. Now, she and her husband invest their time and money in biking with their young family.

If a particular activity becomes a favorite, consider making the investment into that. Those costs meet the real need of caring for yourself.

Whatever you enjoy doing, remember that it is a gift of God. And when you enjoy it with thanksgiving, it can be a form of worship!

*Lord, I'm glad that You're the Lord of
all of life—even of my recreation.*

Friday

ARE YOU HAVING FUN YET?

The LORD has compassion on those who
fear him; for he knows how we are formed,
he remembers that we are dust.
PSALM 103:13–14 NIV

Some women don't take enough time to stop and play. Others suffer from FOMO—fear of missing out. And for every woman anxious that she might be missing out on some fun, many more worry that their children are. Not much true recreation happens if the family calendar is so full that everyone is exhausted and cranky.

Our culture offers more amazing experiences than any one person could enjoy in a lifetime. Planning and pursuing recreation is well worth the time and effort, but every weekend doesn't have to feel like Disneyland.

How many activities can you or your family pursue in a season? Have you considered limiting the number of sports or other activities each child participates in? Have you thought about how much time you spend on your own activities?

Do you have too many or too few outings on your calendar? Why not sit down today and plan something—or cancel an activity or two—so you can truly experience the joy and refreshment of recreation.

Lord, I want to be refreshed and
renewed, not just busy.

Date: ....

Lord, I thank You that recreational activities
engage my mind and body in new ways,
providing much-needed enjoyment and restoration.

5 TOPICS COVERED THIS WEEK:

Monday: re-create outdoors
Tuesday: plan ahead so you can play
Wednesday: find your best fit
Thursday: pay for your play
Friday: are you having fun yet?

3 WAYS RECREATION RESTORES ME:

1...

2...

3...

3 WAYS RECREATION DEPLETES ME:

1...

2...

3...

How I want to respond to these truths:

....

....

....

....

....

....

....

....

....

LORD, HERE'S WHAT'S GOING ON IN MY LIFE RIGHT NOW. . .

OTHER THINGS I NEED TO
SHARE WITH YOU, LORD. . .

Lord, when it comes to this
new life map, I need to. . .

"My purpose is to give them
a rich and satisfying life."
JOHN 10:10 NLT

Thank You, Lord, for
hearing my prayers
and for helping
me take action!
AMEN.

WEEK 18
Entertainment

This week we're going to focus on entertainment. Like you, I'm all for enjoying music, movies, television series, streaming libraries, and apps. My goal? To help you cultivate a new vision for the role of entertainment in your own life.

In our culture, entertainment is everywhere. It's almost impossible to avoid celebrities, athletes, and their work. A lot of entertainment is great, either as a way to relax or be challenged to see the world through new eyes. Some aspects of our entertainment culture, though, require some real discernment.

For the next week, we'll consider principles for approaching entertainment "Christianly." I hope these thoughts will inform your consumption of entertainment while giving you a greater love for the Lord.

Everything good is a gift from God to be enjoyed. I do hope you experience much joy this week!

Whether you eat or drink or whatever you do, do it all for the glory of God.
1 CORINTHIANS 10:31 NIV

Monday

THE BIG PICTURE

> Finally, brothers and sisters, whatever is true,
> whatever is noble, whatever is right, whatever is pure,
> whatever is lovely, whatever is admirable—if anything
> is excellent or praiseworthy—think about such things.
> PHILIPPIANS 4:8 NIV

When I say "the big picture," I don't mean the latest block-buster movie. Let's begin our week by discussing the very important principle of Philippians 4:8.

The apostle Paul's words here encapsulate and elaborate other teachings throughout scripture. Paul also wrote Romans 8:6 ("The mind governed by the flesh is death, but the mind governed by the Spirit is life and peace"), Ephesians 4:17 ("I tell you this, and insist on it in the Lord, that you must no longer live as the Gentiles do, in the futility of their thinking"), and 1 Corinthians 2:16 ("We have the mind of Christ"). And the psalms and proverbs contain many instructions on how to be wise and godly in our thoughts (for example, Psalm 1:2, 63:6, 77:12, 119:15, and 143:5).

The point is simply this: God wants us to engage our minds with Him and His truth. Some forms of entertainment will help us to do that. Others will be neutral, and some will actively oppose the Lord. This week, we'll consider ways of approaching and even redeeming our entertainment.

> *Lord, I want to fill my mind with things that*
> *are good—true, noble, right, and lovely things.*
> *Please guide me in my approach to entertainment.*

Tuesday

A CASE FOR ENTERTAINMENT

*"As some of your own poets have
said, 'We are his offspring.'"*
ACTS 17:28 NIV

Depending on your age and church background, you may have been taught that many forms of entertainment were inappropriate for Christians. Attitudes are much more relaxed these days, but not too long ago, many churches frowned on attending movies. A century or more back, many leading preachers discouraged people from watching theater productions.

Personal convictions on such things are fine (see Romans 14). But it's interesting to note that the apostle Paul was very aware of the entertainment culture of his day. In the verse above, he quotes an Athenian poet; he may have quoted a centuries-old Greek play in 1 Corinthians 15:33; and several times he referenced the sporting events of his world (see 1 Corinthians 9:24, 26; Galatians 2:2, 5:7). Always, Paul used these examples to make some distinctly Christian points.

As you approach your entertainment options, why not do the same thing? Watch, listen, and experience with a goal of seeing Jesus more clearly. I'll have some suggestions for how to do that in the next two readings.

*Lord, please help me to "see" Jesus
today in my entertainment choices.
What would You have me to enjoy?*

Wednesday

APPROACH ENTERTAINMENT THOUGHTFULLY

> We use our powerful God-tools for smashing
> warped philosophies, tearing down barriers
> erected against the truth of God, fitting every
> loose thought and emotion and impulse into
> the structure of life shaped by Christ.
> 2 CORINTHIANS 10:5 MSG

We often turn to entertainment to escape the frustrations of real life. There's value in that, but as Christians we help ourselves by keeping our brains (and spirits) engaged.

Some movies and music and other types of entertainment will support our love and worship of God—and by approaching these thoughtfully, we can learn even more about Him and the life we should live. Some forms of entertainment require more discernment—they represent the ways and values of our world, and a thoughtful approach is to filter their messages through scripture. For example, it may be exciting, from our human perspective, to see a mistreated movie character wreak revenge on the bad guy—but Romans 12:19 clearly says that is God's job, not ours.

As we consume entertainment, may we always be thinking—"fitting every loose thought and emotion and impulse into the structure of life shaped by Christ."

*Lord, I'm thankful for the mind You've given
me. Please keep it engaged with Your
truth, even as I'm being entertained.*

Thursday

BE AWARE OF THEMES

Discretion will protect you,
and understanding will guard you.
PROVERBS 2:11 NIV

Yesterday, I encouraged you to approach entertainment thoughtfully. Today, we'll build upon that idea.

One thing to note as you watch, listen, read, or play, is the theme of the entertainment. What is the underlying message of the movie, song, book, or game? Many times, completely secular entertainments still emphasize Christian themes—of family, duty, forgiveness, hope, courage, love, you name it. That's to be expected, since God wrote the biggest and best story to begin with!

At other times, the themes are negative, nothing you'd want to build your life upon. Even in these cases, though, a thoughtful consideration of the underlying message can remind you of the incredible value of God's Word. Knowing His truth, you don't have to live the kind of hard life so often depicted in media.

Allow your entertainment choices to generate gratitude to God—either for their positive, uplifting messages or for the realization of what He has saved you from.

Lord, may I always appreciate the salvation
I have through Jesus—whether a particular
entertainment celebrates or dismisses it.

Friday
A WORD OF WARNING

Guard your heart above all else,
for it determines the course of your life.
PROVERBS 4:23 NLT

I have offered a positive take on the issue of entertainment because I believe it's one of the many potentially good things God has given us to enjoy. But we need to be honest about its dangers too. Just as medicine or sex or even a fast car can be misused to our harm, so can movies, music, and other diversions.

They're called "diversions" because they divert our attention—and that's where the danger lies. As Christians, we should always keep the Lord in our thoughts. If binge-watching movies or television episodes crowds Him out, or if violence or profanity or sexual content dulls our minds to the teaching of Philippians 4:8, we're inviting danger into our lives. And that's not something we want on our life map!

God wants to be involved in every aspect of life, even our amusements. Ask Him for guidance, and He will gladly answer. Enjoy what He allows, and thank Him for the opportunity to rest and refresh through entertainment.

Lord, I'm grateful for the breaks You give
me from the stresses of life. Help me to honor
You through my entertainment choices.

Date: _____

Lord, everything good is a gift from You to be enjoyed with thanksgiving. Help me to cultivate a vision for the role of entertainment in my life that glorifies You.

5 TOPICS COVERED THIS WEEK:

Monday: the big picture
Tuesday: a case for entertainment
Wednesday: approach entertainment thoughtfully
Thursday: be aware of themes
Friday: a word of warning

3 WAYS ENTERTAINMENT INSPIRES ME:

1..

2..

3..

3 WAYS ENTERTAINMENT MAKES ME STUMBLE:

1..

2..

3..

How I want to respond to these truths:

....

....

....

....

....

....

....

....

....

....

LORD, HERE'S WHAT'S GOING ON IN MY LIFE RIGHT NOW. . .

OTHER THINGS I NEED TO
SHARE WITH YOU, LORD. . .

Lord, when it comes to this
new life map, I need to. . .

God. . .richly gives us all we
need for our enjoyment.
1 TIMOTHY 6:17 NLT

Thank You, Lord, for
hearing my prayers
and for helping
me take action!
AMEN.

WEEK 19
Personal Improvement

We would like personal improvement to be like putting Miracle-Gro on the garden. "Just add prayer and Bible reading!"—and spiritual, mental, and emotional maturity will appear. It doesn't work that way, though. Like trees, human beings need a long time to mature.

The biblical writers picture our lives as brief as flowers. But if we trust in God, we will become as strong and fruitful as trees—to the very end of our lives.

I can't force personal growth on myself or anyone else. But I can pursue it. Through faithful dependence on our source, Jesus Christ, I will begin to see the maturation I long for.

May this week's devotionals cheer you on as you depend ever more upon the Lord.

His delight is in the law of the LORD, and on his law he meditates day and night. He is like a tree planted by streams of water that yields its fruit in its season, and its leaf does not wither. In all that he does, he prospers.

PSALM 1:2–3 ESV

Monday

GROW SPIRITUALLY

So neither the one who plants nor the one who waters
is anything, but only God, who makes things grow.
1 CORINTHIANS 3:7 NIV

I live in a land where berries grow abundantly. We have our own little patch of yellow Himalayan raspberry bushes. They would be fruitless if we didn't trim the canes back severely at the end of each winter. After that, rain, sunshine, and warm weather do all the rest. When the soft and sweet-as-honey berries appear, we waste no time eating and sharing them.

Jesus pictured grapes, not berries, when He described our spiritual growth and relationship with Him (John 15:1–8), but both kind of plants need pruning to produce fruit. Jesus said it, and I've experienced it: God's first job is to trim back the branches and twigs in my life. How I choose to experience that trimming is so important.

Am I resenting my losses or anticipating growth? After that, how do I choose to experience the wind, rain, hail, clouds, and sunshine He sends? Do I see them all as God's good hand of blessing for my spiritual growth and fruitfulness?

Lord, many times I'd rather skip the trimming and
go straight to growth. Please change my mindset
to honor Your wise management of my life.

Tuesday
GROW SOCIALLY

We ought always to give thanks to God for you, brothers, as is right, because your faith is growing abundantly, and the love of every one of you for one another is increasing.
2 THESSALONIANS 1:3 ESV

How many people do you know? Have a number in mind? The figure may or may not be equal to your number of "friends" on Facebook or followers on Instagram. The reality is that all of us have several spheres of relationships, each with differing levels of communication and commitment.

Growing socially is more about quality than quantity. You only have so much time and energy. How will you invest in your relationships?

Here's an idea: purchase some three-by-five-inch index cards. Use them to jot down prayer needs of specific family members and friends. Make a commitment to pray for all of them weekly—or monthly, if you need to start small. Then start casually mentioning, "I pray for you regularly." Then ask, "How can I best pray for you these next couple of weeks?"

Nothing revolutionizes your social life more than intentional, heartfelt prayer for those who mean the most to you.

Lord, the apostle Paul highly valued prayer for others. May I do the same.

Wednesday
GROW MENTALLY

Live a life worthy of the Lord and please him
in every way: bearing fruit in every good
work, growing in the knowledge of God.
COLOSSIANS 1:10 NIV

Time magazine once published an article that indicated many people buy best-selling books without ever reading them. An accompanying chart named a dozen popular books and a best guess of how many people had actually read them. The estimates went as low as one percent!

In other words, collecting best-selling books doesn't equal mental growth—but having no books on your shelves suggests a severe mental famine. We've heard, "Use it or lose it," and that idea certainly applies to our minds!

Even non-readers can enjoy the stimulation of the written word. Why not look for an audio version when someone recommends an impactful book?

Long gone are the days where every home had a family Bible. Yet reading God's Word, the holy scriptures, is what generates fear of the Lord and true wisdom (Job 28:28, Psalm 111:10, Proverbs 1:7, 2:5, 9:10; Ecclesiastes 12:12–14).

Read other good books, certainly. But never neglect the Book of books!

Lord, I thank You for giving us Your Word,
which is more relevant now than ever.

Thursday

GROW EMOTIONALLY

Grow in the grace and knowledge of our
Lord and Savior Jesus Christ. To him
be glory both now and forever!
2 PETER 3:18 NIV

A good friend, Jeannie Clarkson, told my husband and me, "In my counseling practice, I work with lots of people experiencing overwhelming negative emotions—shame, fear, anxiety, or anger, for example—as we all do at times. Everyone, myself included, benefits when we grow our ability to understand and manage our feelings."

Jeannie trains pastors and leaders in "emotional intelligence." She recommends the book *Why Emotions Matter* by Tristen and Jonathan Collins. Jeannie says, "Their book will definitely help if you find yourself struggling or being swept away by negative emotions. You will learn to recognize negative feelings before they get out of hand as well as increase your more positive happy feelings."

Whether or not you consider yourself an "emotional" person, you are. God created you as a complete human being with a mind, body, spirit, and emotions—all connected. The healthier your emotional state, the more you can help others and bring glory to God.

Lord, I know I need to grow emotionally.
Show me how to manage my feelings and honor You.

Friday

GROW VOLITIONALLY

It is God who works in you to will and to
act in order to fulfill his good purpose.
PHILIPPIANS 2:13 NIV

If there's any area of life where we need to depend on the Lord fully and completely, it's in the area of growing volitionally. What does that mean? We all make choices hundreds of times a day. God doesn't scrutinize the color of your socks (or even if they match!). But He does care deeply about your choices for and against His written Word, the Bible. What's more, He cares deeply about your decisions for and against your "neighbors"—including your family and friends and colleagues.

Most decisions we make are benign. Advertising may suggest otherwise, but what you eat or drink at breakfast probably won't register on the Richter scale. What you think about another person at breakfast, or what you say to her, or how you say it—now, those are the kinds of choices God watches.

Here are four ways to grow volitionally: (1) Don't sweat life's little decisions. (2) Do sweat how you impact others. (3) When you blow it, apologize. (4) Trust God and obey Him one day at a time.

*Lord, remind me how my choices impact others—
and my own heart. Change me from the inside out.*

Date: ....

Lord Jesus, personal improvement doesn't come overnight. Instead, it comes through faithful dependence on You, my Creator and Maker.

5 TOPICS COVERED THIS WEEK:

Monday: grow spiritually
Tuesday: grow socially
Wednesday: grow mentally
Thursday: grow emotionally
Friday: grow volitionally

3 WAYS PERSONAL GROWTH EXCITES ME:

1..

2..

3..

3 WAYS PERSONAL GROWTH TROUBLES ME:

1..

2..

3..

How I want to respond to these truths:

....

....

....

....

....

....

....

....

....

LORD, HERE'S WHAT'S GOING ON IN MY LIFE RIGHT NOW. . .

OTHER THINGS I NEED TO
SHARE WITH YOU, LORD. . .

Lord, when it comes to this new life map, I need to. . .

I press on toward the
goal to win the prize for
which God has called me
heavenward in Christ Jesus.
PHILIPPIANS 3:14 NIV

*Thank You, Lord, for
hearing my prayers
and for helping
me take action!*
AMEN.

WEEK 20

Fitness

I like to quip, "Young men should do dangerous things so they have stories to tell when they're older." Young women too—if they want! Climb up mountains or ski down them. Surf big waves or bike long distances. For most of us, time and gravity will eventually slow us down. But whether you're a world-class athlete or you've always been the "take it easy" type, fitness is both crucial and attainable.

Thankfully, it doesn't require dangerous activity and lots of adrenaline. Surprisingly, the core of fitness comes down to a few basics, including good hydration, a healthy diet, intentional breaks, brisk walking, and hand-picked exercises. Gratefully caring for the body God gave you is actually a form of worship.

Physical training is of some value, but godliness has value for all things, holding promise for both the present life and the life to come.

1 TIMOTHY 4:8 NIV

Monday
KEEP HYDRATED

[Jesus said,] "If anyone gives even a cup of
cold water to one of these little ones who
is my disciple, truly I tell you, that person
will certainly not lose their reward."
MATTHEW 10:42 NIV

My husband's friend Wayne mocked the idea of a water back-pack for his hike down and back up the Grand Canyon. He had never used one while climbing North America's highest mountains. Staff at the breakfast café tried to convince him, but Wayne wouldn't be dissuaded. *The canyon, he thought, is only a mile deep.*

Of course, that vertical mile is made up of many miles of switchbacks that slowly take you to the bottom. When Wayne finished his one plastic bottle of water, he tossed it with plans to retrieve it on the way back. He never did—as the sun filled the canyon and the temperature soared, Wayne passed out. Three women later found him unconscious along the trail.

Without water, we'll last only a few hours in a dry, hot climate or a few days in a cooler, wetter place. Yet many of us compromise our fitness by failing to drink enough. When Jesus promised "living water" (John 4:10), He was describing a spiritual blessing. But isn't it instructive that He used *water* as His example?

*Lord, remind me to drink enough water
today. It's one of Your greater gifts!*

Tuesday

MAINTAIN A HEALTHY DIET

*For everything God created is good, and nothing is to
be rejected if it is received with thanksgiving, because
it is consecrated by the word of God and prayer.*
1 TIMOTHY 4:4–5 NIV

When our two older daughters were young teens, they announced they had become vegetarians. David and I agreed to their plan, on three conditions. They needed to help with the cooking, study nutrition, and join their dad in studying what the Bible says about food.

They quickly discovered that God's Word has a lot to say about what we eat! Food is mentioned in the first few chapters of scripture, with meat introduced into the human diet by Genesis 9. The Old Testament books are filled with dietary guidelines for the nation of Israel to stay spiritually separate and physically strong.

In the New Testament, Jesus made it clear that nothing we eat can make us more or less holy. He also said to eat whatever is placed before us (Luke 10:8). Both of our daughters later did exactly that while traveling in Africa and China.

God doesn't give us one right way to eat. But if you want to eat to please Him, do it with self-control and gratitude.

*Lord, I'm grateful for the food You provide.
Please help me to eat wisely and well.*

Wednesday

TAKE INTENTIONAL BREAKS

"[Ruth] said, 'Please let me glean and gather among
the sheaves behind the harvesters.' She came into
the field and has remained here from morning
till now, except for a short rest in the shelter."
RUTH 2:7 NIV

In Bible times, people took intentional breaks as we see in the story of Ruth above. Sometimes the break was an evening nap in a boat (Mark 4:38). Sometimes it was an outdoor nap after eating (1 Kings 19:6). Sometimes it meant sitting in the shade in the heat of the day (Genesis 18:1). Thanks to the examples of Ruth, Jesus, Elijah, and Abraham, we're encouraged to take breaks too—each in our own way.

When I worked part-time, I usually ate at my desk to make the most of my few hours at the office. Now that I work full-time, I intentionally take my lunch to the staff kitchen and eat at the table, and I coax my colleagues to join me. I remind them that, with our stressful work, we need to take breaks to stay sane, stable, and productive. Are any of us more capable than Jesus?

*Lord, please help me to take intentional breaks
from my work. Refresh and renew me.*

Thursday
ENJOY WALKING

> "These words that I command you today shall be
> on your heart. You shall teach them diligently to
> your children, and shall talk of them when you sit
> in your house, and when you walk by the way."
> DEUTERONOMY 6:6–7 ESV

I admire runners and joggers. I cheer my friends and family members when they cross the finish line of their latest 5K, 10K, or marathon. I'm not built for running, but someday I might just try a 5K—as long as I can walk it!

Runners in biblical times included Joseph (when fleeing temptation), David (in combat and fleeing from Saul), and Elijah (racing King Ahab's chariot back to the capital). And don't forget that Jesus told a famous story about a gentleman running to embrace his long-lost prodigal son.

Mostly, however, God's Word talks about walking. During three years of public ministry, Jesus walked through the territory of every tribe of Israel except one. As a child, He trekked the roads back to Nazareth when He returned with Mary and Joseph from Egypt. Later, Jesus, His parents, family, and community journeyed by foot to Jerusalem for the Passover and other important festivals.

Fitness experts expound the advantages of walking. You'll find physical benefits, but also refreshment for your mind and soul.

Lord, help me to add walking to my daily routine.
I want to benefit my body, mind, and spirit.

Friday

USE HAND-PICKED EXERCISES

Everyone who competes in the games goes into strict
training. They do it to get a crown that will not last,
but we do it to get a crown that will last forever.

1 CORINTHIANS 9:25 NIV

Throughout history, exercise happened primarily through the vigor of daily living: hauling water, chopping wood, tending gardens, washing clothes, and making things. The Greeks had the luxury to put on competitions to demonstrate athletic prowess, but then, like now, few people are Olympians.

Today, we know more than ever about the complex design of the human body—and how to care for it. For some people, exercise is about being as strong and fit as possible. For others, it means using specific exercises to address physical pain or challenges.

My chiropractor always encourages me to start with two simple stretches each morning. Over the past year, I've added several more to my morning routine to address pain in my hip and back. I'm not winning any medals, but I can walk again without pain.

Find ways to take care of your own body. God's given you just one—so make it last!

*Lord, thank You for the incredible design
and capability of my body. Guide me in
taking the best possible care of it.*

Date: _____

Lord, some people want an adrenaline rush, but I know that I need to focus on the core of fitness, including moderate physical activity day after day.

5 TOPICS COVERED THIS WEEK:

Monday: drink lots of water
Tuesday: maintain a healthy diet
Wednesday: take intentional breaks
Thursday: enjoy walks
Friday: use hand-picked exercises

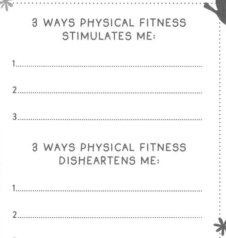

3 WAYS PHYSICAL FITNESS STIMULATES ME:

1. ....
2. ....
3. ....

3 WAYS PHYSICAL FITNESS DISHEARTENS ME:

1. ....
2. ....
3. ....

How I want to respond to these truths:

LORD, HERE'S WHAT'S GOING ON IN MY LIFE RIGHT NOW. . .

OTHER THINGS I NEED TO
SHARE WITH YOU, LORD. . .

Lord, when it comes to this
new life map, I need to. . .

Work with your hands,
just as we told you, so that
your daily life may win
the respect of outsiders
and so that you will not be
dependent on anybody.
1 THESSALONIANS 4:11–12 NIV

Thank You, Lord, for
hearing my prayers
and for helping
me take action!
AMEN.

WEEK 21
Travel

Some people visit all the national parks, and others drive to Grandma's once a year. Some long for tropical paradises; others can't wait to visit historical sites. Some travel out of curiosity, to make connections, or simply to celebrate life.

If you step outside your state, you can experience your great country. If you step outside your country, you can get a bigger taste of this amazing planet. The most important step is to go!

As a young married couple, David and I knew a wealthy older widow whose husband had promised to take her all over the world when he retired. But he didn't retire until he was seventy-five; he took her on a single cruise and shortly thereafter passed away. We determined not to make that same mistake.

As a couple, David and I have many great memories of trips we've taken around the world. You won't regret the travels you plan this week.

He makes me lie down in green pastures, he leads me
beside quiet waters, he refreshes my soul. He guides
me along the right paths for his name's sake.

PSALM 23:2–3 NIV

Monday

WHERE TO GO AND HOW TO GET THERE

*I will instruct you and teach you in the way you should
go; I will counsel you with my loving eye on you.*
PSALM 32:8 NIV

Is there somewhere you've always wanted to go? Dust off
that dream today. What would be special about visiting that
place? Are there intriguing connections to family, history,
literature, or music?

Why not begin planning a trip for the coming year? Revisit
your travel dreams periodically, with the goal of actually going.

Remember, travel isn't only a flight or cruise to an exotic
location. Road trips offer many joys of their own. And don't
be afraid to travel by bus—the ride can be inexpensive, and it's
usually quiet. Taking the train might be an even better option.
Railroad tracks often provide stunning views.

Now is the time to dream and plan. As Dr. Seuss famously
said, "Oh, the places you'll go."

*Lord, I thank You for promising to be with
me wherever I go. May I experience You in
parts of Your world that are new to me.*

Tuesday

TRAVEL TIPS

> "The LORD himself goes before you and
> will be with you; he will never leave you
> nor forsake you. Do not be afraid."
>
> DEUTERONOMY 31:8 NIV

Wherever you go, find something to appreciate, even if it's less than you expected. Our tiny hotel room in Paris didn't provide the best night's sleep, but we were there to have new experiences—not replicate home.

Our friend Drenda travels the world, but her most treasured memory is celebrating her husband Don's birthday in Rome. They sat outside on a restaurant patio, drank espresso, and watched people for two hours in front of the Pantheon. You don't experience thousands of years of history like that back home, so take advantage of every moment.

Sign up for tours, but not all of them. City tours offer insights and take you places you might not find on your own. But it's also good to leave plenty of time just to wander.

And be sure to enjoy the cuisine. You haven't experienced a culture until you've tasted the food. Use discretion (don't drink the water!), but do try out local dishes. Oh, and pack the Pepto Bismol.

Wherever you go, remember that God is with you—cheering you on!

*Lord, I'd like to know more of the world You have
created. Guide me into the places You want me to see.*

Wednesday

TRAVEL MISTAKES

The LORD makes firm the steps of
the one who delights in him.
PSALM 37:23 NIV

Tips to minimize travel mistakes:

Don't dress to impress when you travel. Traveling light costs less—and leaves room for souvenirs.

Allow time for spontaneous adventures. After all, you might meet someone who invites you to a local event. Join in the fun!

Don't try to visit too many destinations. You can't see a tenth of all the museums in Washington, DC, in four days. And don't try to see Rome, Paris, Florence, or Venice in a week.

Remember: "Everyone vacations in their own way." Talk ahead of time about what you're most looking forward to doing. Do you love having a leisurely breakfast and then reading for an hour, or do you prefer getting up and exploring right away? Make sure you travel with family or friends who have the physical health, stamina, and ability to enjoy the activities you want to do. Take into account preferences for sleeping and eating schedules—and just how flexible each person is. Allow for time for people to do their own thing.

The biggest travel mistake? Not going!

*Lord, please give me wisdom and flexibility to
travel well—to get the most from my experience.*

Thursday

PLAN AND PAY FOR TRAVEL

*If I rise on the wings of the dawn, if I settle on
the far side of the sea, even there your hand will
guide me, your right hand will hold me fast.*
PSALM 139:9–10 NIV

If you plan ahead, you can travel more often than you might guess. Why not start a travel savings account? If you use direct deposit from your paycheck, designate perhaps thirty dollars for this account. After a few months, consider increasing that amount.

Learn to use online booking sites and find the ones that work best for you. Consider booking flights to secondary airports—sometimes flights are much less expensive if you're willing to travel, say, a hundred miles by car.

When using small airlines, watch for hidden costs, and allow for the greater possibility of delayed and cancelled flights. Using these airlines for solo or unhurried travel makes more sense than when you're traveling with children or on a tight schedule.

Of course, you can always take a road trip, packing your own food to save money. Visit or swap houses with friends in different areas of the country. There are plenty of travel options—the important thing is to get out and see God's world!

*Lord, please help me to budget carefully and set
aside money for future travel. I want a bigger
perspective on the world You've given us.*

Friday

MAKE TRAVEL MEANINGFUL

The LORD will watch over your coming and going both now and forevermore.
PSALM 121:8 NIV

Travel takes you away from your everyday responsibilities and transports you somewhere new. Whether your trip is exciting, educational, or restful, it promises more than just a good time. Travel expands your perspectives about other people.

Make travel more meaningful by studying the places you plan to visit. Read their history, but also check out their current challenges. Consider how you can support the economy during your visit. Meet some local residents. David took our younger son on a road trip down the Oregon coast. Ben loved visiting small towns off the beaten path so he could ask shop owners for their stories.

Travel to serve. Helping to build a small home in an impoverished town blesses you just as much as the receiving family. Visiting missionaries and seeing their world means so much to them. Give the gift of listening and helping with physical tasks or ministry. And still see the sights!

Best of all, return home with a bigger sense of God's heart for the world.

Lord, I thank You that I can be blessed and a blessing when I travel.

Date: ....

Lord, I want to dream, plan, schedule, travel,
and return home with a greater appreciation for this
world and a bigger sense of Your heart for people.

5 TOPICS COVERED THIS WEEK:

Monday: where to go and how to get there
Tuesday: travel tips
Wednesday: travel mistakes
Thursday: plan and pay for travel
Friday: make travel meaningful

3 WAYS TRAVEL APPEALS TO ME:

1. ....
2. ....
3. ....

3 WAYS TRAVEL CONCERNS ME:

1. ....
2. ....
3. ....

How I want to respond to these truths:

....

....

....

....

....

....

....

....

....

....

LORD, HERE'S WHAT'S GOING ON IN MY LIFE RIGHT NOW. . .

OTHER THINGS I NEED TO
SHARE WITH YOU, LORD. . .

Lord, when it comes to this
new life map, I need to. . .

We plan the way we want
to live, but only GOD
makes us able to live it.
PROVERBS 16:9 MSG

Thank You, Lord, for
hearing my prayers
and for helping
me take action!
AMEN.

WEEK 22
Finances, Part 1

The apostle Paul lived in a world like ours—rich in culture, education, art, and luxuries. Without the Internet, television, or even mass-market books, he knew what the Roman world had to offer. Still, Paul could say, "I have learned to be content whatever the circumstances" (Philippians 4:11 NIV). Don't miss that word *learned*.

As a younger man, a member of the Pharisees, Paul (then known as Saul) was probably wealthy—likely a man who loved money (see Luke 16:14). As an apostle, however, he repeatedly lost his possessions to theft, riots, imprisonment, and shipwreck. He consistently worked hard to provide for his own needs and the needs of others. He also gratefully accepted gifts for his needs. Paul made himself at home both in prison and on the estates of his friends. He lived out Philippians 4:11 for decades—and we can too.

It's clear that Paul isn't against wealth. He enjoyed everything with gratitude and without guilt: "I know what it is to be in need, and I know what it is to have plenty. I have learned the secret of being content in any and every situation" (Philippians 4:12 NIV).

Like Paul, we start with an attitude of gratitude. This week, we'll explore the next steps of daily financial wisdom.

Wealth gained hastily will dwindle, but whoever gathers little by little will increase it.

PROVERBS 13:11 ESV

Monday

NET INCOME OVER TIME

Make it your goal to live a quiet life,
minding your own business and working.
1 THESSALONIANS 4:11 NLT

Wealth—or simply having enough money—doesn't happen automatically or magically. Financial well-being is like healthy eating. The basics are simple and inescapable: managing income and expenses.

Today, we focus on income. Gross income is what you earn before deductions. Net income is what you take home after taxes, benefit cost-sharing, and miscellaneous fees.

Do you know your current gross and net? If not, look up your latest pay stub or flip back to last year's W-2. It's important to know exactly what your monthly net income is, as well as your monthly expenses.

When your net income is greater than expenses, month after month and year after year, good things are happening for you and your family. It means no cash flow problems, extra money always on hand for emergencies, growing prosperity. You'll have healthy savings and a growing retirement account.

Bottom line: Exercise and strengthen your contentment "muscles" by consistently spending less than your net income.

Lord, I thank You for the ability to earn
income and spend wisely. Help me to
carefully mind what You've given me.

Tuesday

NET INCOME STREAMS

Remember the LORD your God, for it is he who
gives you the ability to produce wealth.
DEUTERONOMY 8:18 NIV

In today's on-demand world, anyone with an extra room, car, time, skills, or stuff can pursue income streams via any number of online services. It just takes a few smarts.

One friend works from home and also rents her downstairs as travel lodging to make additional money. Some other friends switched their upstairs rental apartment to travel lodging, assuming it would create increased income—but they found the intensive labor of cleaning the apartment after each guest was stealing time and energy from other, more important parts of life. They could hire out the cleaning, but that cut into their profits. Now, they're trying out other options to maximize their income.

When you need more income, seek it out—but beware of increasing your hours or stress. If a promotion or new job takes a while to gain, that's okay. Better to wait than to make a costly mistake.

*Lord, You give me the ability to produce wealth.
Please help me to use that ability wisely.*

Wednesday

FIRST EXPENSES

Remember the words of the Lord Jesus:
"It is more blessed to give than to receive."
ACTS 20:35 NLT

When you create a budget, at the top is space for income. Below that, you'll capture expenses.

The first expense category is involuntary—it includes federal, state, regional and local taxes and fees.

The second expense category may or may not be voluntary. For example, employer-employee benefit cost-sharing includes health insurance and retirement contributions. If your employer matches the latter by a strong percentage, make sure you add a voluntary contribution of your own!

The third expense is completely voluntary, and it reflects your faith and trust in God and His Word. Such expenses include tithes and offerings to your local church and its missionaries.

Giving comes in many other forms, as well. Through the years my husband and I have made it a priority to sponsor one or more needy children overseas through Compassion International.

As the Lord leads, we also love to do extra giving, like paying for a new water heater for a family down the street. David and I also keep a hundred-dollar bill in our wallets "just in case." We believe, as Jesus said, giving is more blessed than receiving!

*Lord, thank You for the reminder to give.
Increase my sensitivity and generosity.*

Thursday

MONTHLY EXPENSES

*"Won't you first sit down and estimate the
cost to see if you have enough money?"*
LUKE 14:28 NIV

On your personal budget sheet, directly under EXPENSES are two categories: BEFORE NET and AFTER NET.

BEFORE NET includes taxes, fees, benefit cost-sharing, and anything else deducted from your take-home pay. AFTER NET includes two more categories: MONTHLY and DAILY.

Monthly expenses to factor in to your budget include insurance policy costs and your rent or mortgage. The latter should include a prorated amount for the upkeep of your home and yard. (Words of wisdom: don't take on debt to remodel your kitchen or install a new roof. Instead, over time, set aside money each month toward such future expenses.)

Your budget should also list your monthly car payments, student loans, and any other payments. . .as well as charges you've incurred on your credit card and bank account.

And then there are the utility payments: oil, propane, natural gas, electricity, water, garbage, recycling, Internet, phone, and the like. Prorate any that are billed bimonthly or quarterly. The more you can reduce your monthly expenses, the more you'll have to put toward more important things. Christians have plenty of those.

*Lord, I'm glad You know every part of my
budget in detail. Help me to do the same!*

Friday
DAILY EXPENSES

"I have not coveted anyone's silver or gold
or clothing. You yourselves know that these
hands of mine have supplied my own needs
and the needs of my companions."
ACTS 20:33–34 NIV

Paul isn't speaking against silver or gold, and he certainly has no complaint with clothing! But we all know that money and things can be very attractive to our human nature.

We enjoy seeing and owning such things. But can we afford them? And will we be content (as the apostle was) when our possessions are lost due to wear-and-tear, accident, theft, or worse?

For many of us, accumulating nice, quality things happens after we've learned to control our daily expenses. One key in doing that is to track every expenditure you make. You have to know what you have and where it's going to be able to truly plan for the future. If you're married, you want to be on the same page with your husband (figuratively) and tracking everything you each spend (literally). Numerous apps make this easier than ever, but a spreadsheet or old-fashioned notebook works as well.

You won't have to do this forever—just long enough to develop your understanding of expenses and more carefully guide your choices.

Lord, You know all of my wants and needs.
Help me to know the difference between them.

Date: _____

Lord, I want to own this conviction: "Godliness with contentment is great gain" (1 Timothy 6:6 NIV). What a difference that conviction could make in my life now—and for years to come!

5 TOPICS COVERED THIS WEEK:

Monday: monthly net income
Tuesday: income streams
Wednesday: first expenses
Thursday: monthly expenses
Friday: daily expenses

3 WAYS A BUDGET CAN HELP ME:

1. ....

2. ....

3. ....

3 WAYS A BUDGET CAN FRUSTRATE ME:

1. ....

2. ....

3. ....

How I want to respond to these truths:

....

....

....

....

....

....

....

....

....

....

LORD, HERE'S WHAT'S GOING ON IN MY LIFE RIGHT NOW. . .

OTHER THINGS I NEED TO
SHARE WITH YOU, LORD. . .

Lord, when it comes to this
new life map, I need to. . .

Keep your lives free from
the love of money and be
content with what you
have, because God has
said, "Never will I leave you;
never will I forsake you."
HEBREWS 13:5 NIV

Thank You, Lord, for
hearing my prayers
and for helping
me take action!
AMEN.

WEEK 23
Finances, Part 1

Experience is the best teacher—*especially other people's experiences.* This is doubly true when it comes to finances. Skip other weeks in this book, but not this one! God wants you to "act smart" by applying knowledge, discernment, understanding, and wisdom to your finances. Your life is too short to waste money.

A dozen individuals and couples used this week's financial advice for a year and reported saving tens of thousands of dollars. You're sure to come out way ahead too!

We'll discuss smart ways to find a financial advisor, to purchase insurance, to avoid high-rate debt, to correct financial mistakes, and to deal with catastrophic medical crises.

By week's end, you'll have the knowledge to reap substantial financial rewards for a lifetime.

The blessing of the LORD makes rich, and he adds no sorrow with it.
PROVERBS 10:22 ESV

Monday

FIND A FINANCIAL ADVISOR

Wisdom is found in those who take advice.
PROVERBS 13:10 NIV

Throughout this book, I've been offering insights into many life topics, including your finances, and I'll continue to do so. But your specific situation will always be best served by a financial advisor who knows you personally.

When I say "financial advisor," I don't necessarily mean a licensed professional. If you have some resources and the wherewithal to pay for a respected and recommended professional, then certainly do so. But until you reach that point, you may find some great, free advice from a parent or relative, or an older businesswoman at church, or some other successful individual you know. They can provide wise insights on issues like buying versus renting a home, how and when and where to purchase a car, and what kinds of investments may be tailor-made for your situation.

We often think we can "go it alone," but the life experience of older women we know and trust can be a huge advantage to our own futures. Plus, they'll probably enjoy sharing their insights!

Lord, may I always be a woman who takes advice—
especially in this important area of finances.

Tuesday

BUY ESSENTIAL INSURANCE COVERAGE

For the protection of wisdom is like the protection
of money, and the advantage of knowledge is that
wisdom preserves the life of him who has it.
ECCLESIASTES 7:12 ESV

Not all insurance policies are created equal. You want to choose the companies and policies that best fit your needs. Thankfully, you probably need to buy only five policies.

First, health insurance. Co-pays don't matter quite as much as deductibles do. Know what you're getting and how much it will cost you.

Second, disability insurance. No one plans to turn fifty or sixty and suddenly become disabled, but that can happen. Decades ago, my husband and a friend both bought disability insurance policies—and ended up needing them. Gordon's policy was great. David's only paid five hundred dollars a month. Ouch!

Third, term life insurance. Look for a low monthly price that's locked in for the next twenty or thirty years. After a few years, if you're building a family, it's wise to buy a second policy.

Fourth, auto insurance. Buy comprehensive, not collision.

Fifth, home-owners insurance. Make sure "flood" is covered in case, for example, a dishwasher hose springs a leak. Water, like fire, creates a lot of costly damage in a hurry.

Lord, may I always trust You—but also
prepare prudently for the future. Give me
wisdom as I consider insurance.

Wednesday

FLEE HIGH-RATE LOANS

*The rich rule over the poor, and the
borrower is slave to the lender.*
PROVERBS 22:7 NIV

Loan costs can vary dramatically. So you need to have a plan to either avoid or diligently pay off any high-rate loans.

Even if the interest rate starts at 0 percent, never use cash advances from credit cards to boost the size of your proposed house down payment. There's no way you'll be able to pay off that much money before you're hammered with 23 percent to 30 percent interest. Suddenly, you no longer owe $12,000. Instead, you owe $18,000 and then $23,000 and are hopelessly upside down financially.

Don't let that happen! Except for your husband and kids, everything in your house needs a price tag. Sell as much as you can to apply the money to your worst loan. Then sell more stuff to pay off any other high-rate loan. If necessary, take a second job for a while to knock out this kind of debt.

One final word: never co-sign someone else's loan. Nearly 90 percent of the time you'll end up paying a terrible loan for their car, or boat, or whatever. Just a word to the wise.

*Lord, You have warned me against becoming a slave
to high-rate loans. Help me to handle my money
wisely, save patiently, and avoid wasteful situations.*

Thursday

CORRECT SMALL FINANCIAL MISTAKES

> Then [Jesus] said to them, "Watch out! Be on
> your guard against all kinds of greed; life does
> not consist in an abundance of possessions."
> LUKE 12:15 NIV

When you make a small financial mistake, don't ignore it. Instead, take immediate action to un-make it.

If you've just bought something you realize you can't afford, return it or exchange it for something you can. If you've incurred a first-time overdraft charge, drop by your bank, apologize, promise it will never happen again, and ask, "This one time, is there any way this overdraft charge could be reversed?" The phrase "This one time" is crucial. So is the phrase "Is there any way. . . ?" If the answer is no, don't say anything. Just silently count to ten. The teller may study your eyes, go talk with the manager, and say "Yes, this one time." If you've incurred a first-time late payment fee, follow the same guidance online or over the phone.

It never hurts to ask.

Lord, give me wisdom in making my financial
decisions. . .but if I do the wrong thing, prompt
me to un-make that mistake immediately.

Friday

RESPONDING TO HUGE HOSPITAL DEBTS

*God is able to bless you abundantly, so that
in all things at all times, having all that you
need, you will abound in every good work.*
2 Corinthians 9:8 niv

If you're ever hit with catastrophic medical bills, don't immediately think bankruptcy. Come back to this book and reread this page. And feel free to share this information with any family members or friends who find themselves in this situation.

As I write this, America has slightly more than 2,900 community hospitals. The IRS recognizes 59 percent of them as non-profit. This includes the majority of hospitals with religious terms in their names, words such as Adventist, Beth, Holy, Providence, Sacred, Saint, Samaritan, Sinai, and Sister.

These hospitals often have a benevolence fund, sometimes overseen by a related charitable foundation. Each is required to give away a certain amount of money every year. Sometimes those funds are put into medical research, buildings, equipment, and staff. Other funds are used to help people who find it difficult, if not impossible, to pay their hospital bills.

What a relief—and what a great reminder of the way God forgives us.

*Lord, I'm grateful that You are a forgiving God—
and that You encourage others to follow Your example.*

Date: _____

Lord, life is too short to waste money. Help me to
"act smart" by applying knowledge, discernment,
understanding, and wisdom to my finances.

5 TOPICS COVERED THIS WEEK:

Monday: find a financial advisor
Tuesday: buy essential insurance coverage
Wednesday: flee high-rate loans
Thursday: correct small financial mistakes
Friday: responding to huge hospital debts

3 WAYS MONEY MANAGEMENT EXCITES ME:

1. ....

2. ....

3. ....

3 WAYS MONEY MANAGEMENT FRUSTRATES ME:

1. ....

2. ....

3. ....

**How I want to respond
to these truths:**

LORD, HERE'S WHAT'S GOING ON IN MY LIFE RIGHT NOW. . .

....

....

....

....

....

OTHER THINGS I NEED TO
SHARE WITH YOU, LORD. . .

....

....

....

....

....

Lord, when it comes to this
new life map, I need to. . .

....

....

....

....

....

....

"For where your
treasure is, there your
heart will be also."
MATTHEW 6:21 NIV

*Thank You, Lord, for
hearing my prayers
and for helping
me take action!*
AMEN.

WEEK 24
Giving Back, Part 1

Jesus rarely made statements that are easy to believe. Take His words, "You're far happier giving than getting" (Acts 20:35 MSG). Too good to be true? Well, actually, lots of scientifically backed research has documented this counterintuitive reality.

"Giving back" includes volunteer service, community leadership, financial contributions, and relational support. Among the many benefits that you'll enjoy are personal happiness, lowered stress, and an improved immune system. Givers report greater satisfaction with life, more meaning in life, more friends and stronger relationships. They know they've helped to make others happier!

Want some more benefits to giving back? How about a more positive outlook on life, improved mental health, deeper contentment, higher self-esteem, and improved spiritual vitality. And don't forget the eternal rewards.

Never be lacking in zeal, but keep your
spiritual fervor, serving the Lord.
ROMANS 12:11 NIV

Monday

SERVE AT YOUR CHURCH

*Always give yourselves fully to the work
of the Lord, because you know that your
labor in the Lord is not in vain.*
1 CORINTHIANS 15:58 NIV

When David started attending our current church many years ago, he fell in love with the people and quickly volunteered to serve. "We don't do it that way," he was told. "Just sit back and be part of the church family for six months. Then let's see where you might serve."

He ended up going to a second church to work with their youth group during that time. Looking back, he realized he should have given much more priority to "be part of the church family." After David and I were married, we've made up for his impulsiveness every year since.

Become an active member of your church, pray about where you can serve, and then ask someone in leadership for guidance and direction. You may try serving in one or two different ministries before you find just where you fit best. That's okay. God will use the experience to grow you and bless others, no matter how "successful" you feel.

God gifted you to serve. Always make sure you are doing your part.

*Lord, I want to be part of my church family by serving,
not just attending. Show me where you want me.*

Tuesday

LIVE LIKE A LEADER

*The elders who direct the affairs of the church
well are worthy of double honor, especially
those whose work is preaching and teaching.*
1 TIMOTHY 5:17 NIV

God wants every believer to live like a leader. In three scripture passages (1 Timothy 3:1–7, Titus 1:5–9, and 1 Peter 5:1–4), we're told that elders care for, shepherd, pastor, lead, and oversee the local church. These leaders are recognized with official titles, but many other leaders and servants in the church aren't. They live like elders, regardless of age, education, or public recognition.

Living like leaders, women of faith know and learn to teach the truths of the Word of God. This can include leading Bible studies, teaching children, participating in church policy committees, or simply counseling struggling friends. In these ways, every woman can protect the church from false teachers.

Just as importantly, leaders pray for their brothers and sisters, anoint those who are sick, and visit the imprisoned. In other words, they embody the good news of Jesus Christ as they serve in every sphere of life—as wives, mothers, employees, school volunteers, or public officials. Every Christian woman can maintain a good reputation in her community.

*Lord, I want to live up to the qualifications of leaders
in Your church, no matter what my role or position.*

Wednesday

GIVE TO YOUR CHURCH

*Each of you should give what you have decided
in your heart to give, not reluctantly or under
compulsion, for God loves a cheerful giver.*
2 CORINTHIANS 9:7 NIV

If you grew up in a churchgoing family, you may remember taking coins from your allowance to put in the offering plate. If you've only recently starting attending church, maybe you're not so sure what the offering is all about That's okay—even many long-time, committed Christians haven't budgeted for regular giving to their church.

Television preachers are often too pushy about money, so many local pastors hesitate to teach on giving. They don't want to enhance a negative stereotype. But God does call Christians to support their local church—and not just when they feel like it or for special projects, but in a consistent, dependable way.

Our church gets by on a tight budget. I might not think my own giving contributes that much, but joined with the regular gifts of others, the church is enabled to minister to its people and our community. What really matters is your decision to give regularly and cheerfully to God's work.

*Lord, please give me a heart willing to
give from what You've given me.*

Thursday

DONATE TO THE BENEVOLENCE FUND

*"In everything I did, I showed you that by this
kind of hard work we must help the weak,
remembering the words the Lord Jesus himself
said: 'It is more blessed to give than to receive.'"*

ACTS 20:35 NIV

When David and I were starting our family, I was involved in a crash that left me uninjured, but our car totaled. The insurance settlement was far too small to purchase another vehicle, but almost immediately a woman at church loaned us her extra car. Two Sundays later we received a twenty-five-hundred-dollar benevolence gift. God's people are generous!

Our church has two benevolence funds: the first is for church members, the second for outside requests from the community. Both funds distribute thousands of dollars annually. Believe me, someone is always in need.

Churches generally don't talk a lot about their benevolence funds. But they can be vital to many people. Why not ask your pastor if your church has one—and if it needs more donations to keep it strong?

*Lord, please help me to meet needs—whether
individually or through my church's benevolent
fund. May my generosity point people to Jesus!*

Friday

SUPPORT ONE OF YOUR MISSIONARIES

These women were helping to support
[Jesus and the Twelve] out of their own means.
LUKE 8:3 NIV

Not every church sends out missionaries from its own congregation. Our medium-sized church, however, has been something of an overachiever in that regard. Well over a dozen of our close friends have been sent as missionaries to Africa, Asia, Europe, and Latin America. David and I contribute to their support through our local church, and then we help roll out the red carpet when they come home on furloughs.

Many churches contribute to the support of missionaries sent out by other churches. Those missionaries may visit only once every few years, but modern technology makes it easy to keep in touch via email, social media, phone calls, and video conferencing.

As God leads you, sign up to receive the newsletters from your favorite missionaries. Be sure to connect with them via email and social media. As you get to know each other better, contribute funds via your church for their support. Such financial gifts are "acceptable and pleasing to God" (Philippians 4:18 NLT).

Lord, please show me a missionary to support,
both with money and with prayers and correspondence.
Use my gifts to make a difference around the world.

Date: _____

Lord, I thank You for the many benefits of
"giving back": greater happiness, lower stress,
greater satisfaction, more friends, and eternal rewards.

5 TOPICS COVERED THIS WEEK:

Monday: serve at your church
Tuesday: live like a leader
Wednesday: give to your church
Thursday: donate to the benevolence fund
Friday: support one of your missionaries

3 WAYS GIVING BACK APPEALS TO ME:

1. ....
2. ....
3. ....

3 WAYS GIVING BACK CONCERNS ME:

1. ....
2. ....
3. ....

How I want to respond to these truths:

LORD, HERE'S WHAT'S GOING ON IN MY LIFE RIGHT NOW. . .

OTHER THINGS I NEED TO
SHARE WITH YOU, LORD. . .

Lord, when it comes to this
new life map, I need to. . .

And this same God who
takes care of me will
supply all your needs
from his glorious riches,
which have been given
to us in Christ Jesus.
PHILIPPIANS 4:19 NLT

Thank You, Lord, for
hearing my prayers
and for helping
me take action!
AMEN.

WEEK 25
Giving Back, Part 2

This past week we highlighted the many benefits of generosity, whether you are serving at your church, living like an elder, or contributing to your church offering, benevolence fund, and missionaries.

This week, we'll explore five even more active ideas for giving back: visiting a missionary overseas, hosting a refugee family, sponsoring a needy child, serving as a foster parent, and considering adoption.

In each of these areas, you may have to stretch way outside your comfort zone and depend on the Lord more than any other time in your life. These are challenging tasks! But the experiences will add amazing highlights in your life map.

David and I are not wealthy, and often have had to scrape by—but we always felt the Lord prompting us to step out in faith. I hope that's your experience five times over.

"Test me in this," says the Lord Almighty, "and see if I will not throw open the floodgates of heaven and pour out so much blessing that there will not be room enough to store it."

MALACHI 3:10 NIV

Monday

VISIT A MISSIONARY OVERSEAS

*Leaving the next day, we reached Caesarea and stayed
at the house of Philip the evangelist, one of the Seven.*
ACTS 21:8 NIV

Years ago, David and I were chatting with friends at a Christmas party about their upcoming summer trip. Greg and Gwen were leading a team to visit three of our church's missionaries on the Pacific coast of Peru. Wow. We said we would love to take a trip like that. It turned out that Gwen had just learned she was pregnant—so David and I did go, in Greg and Gwen's place! The trip proved challenging on many levels, but we look back and see how God used the time to bless the church there.

More recent trips to visit our church's missionaries have been much more intentional on our part. We always ask ahead and plan the trips around the missionary family's schedule and needs. We ask for a list of their hard-to-get items, then fill our suitcases full. We come prepared to share testimonies, teach, or do projects. On some occasions, we're there just to do life together.

When you visit missionaries where they live, you're giving the gift of money, time, and yourself. Why not start praying about which of your church's missionaries you might visit?

*Lord, put a missionary on my heart, and show
me if and how I should plan a visit.*

Tuesday

HOST A REFUGEE COUPLE

> There was an estate nearby that belonged to Publius,
> the chief official of the island. He welcomed us to
> his home and showed us generous hospitality.
>
> ACTS 28:7 NIV

After the fall of Saigon, Vietnam, in 1975, my parents hosted three different refugee families fleeing communism to come to the United States. They knew little or no English, and they had no idea how life worked here in America—but they wanted to learn, and fast! In time, each family became successful in its own right. What a joy to see their children thrive and start families of their own. They've brought such joy to my family through the years.

Some refugee couples and families live for a while with sponsors, but most now receive their own government-subsidized apartments. Most of them have enough money to purchase what they need to live on. What they really need are American families who welcome them, help them practice English, and answer their questions. Our family's motto: There are no dumb questions—especially if your guests ask why you're being so helpful. What an opportunity to share the gospel!

Lord, open my heart to needy people
from around the world, and show me
how I might become a help to them.

Wednesday

SPONSOR A NEEDY CHILD

Defend the weak and the fatherless;
uphold the cause of the poor and the oppressed.
PSALM 82:3 NIV

Years ago, David and I were introduced to Compassion International. Many organizations offer child sponsorship, but we've done the research and found this organization to be outstanding in providing for a child's basic needs and education in the context of their own family and community. What a privilege to invest in one child's life and see him or her grow up to be a strong and capable adult. We're humbled when our sponsored child says, "I love you and I'm praying for you."

It's easy to sign up to sponsor a needy child. Just be sure you're ready to make a long-term commitment. It's not a huge amount of money, but once you sponsor a specific child, it's an expense you don't want to cut.

Today sponsorship is easier and more interactive than ever. David and I automatically have monthly payments deducted from our checking account. And we use the organization's web site to correspond with each child, send and receive photos and artwork, and make special contributions to their family for birthdays and Christmas.

Knowing how Jesus loved children, it just seems right.

Lord, please bless the needy children of the world—
and let me know how I might play a part in that.

Thursday

SERVE AS A FOSTER PARENT

Learn to do right; seek justice. Defend the
oppressed. Take up the cause of the fatherless.
ISAIAH 1:17 NIV

David and I had just signed up for foster parent training when we received a call from a caseworker. Could we take two neglected girls, ages five and eight, right now? David was on a business trip, so I called him. We agreed. Nine months later, our foster girls were reunited with their birth mom. Today those girls are married with families of their own.

Every day in America more than 420,000 children are in foster care. They didn't ask to be placed there. Instead, their parents or guardians somehow neglected or abused them. These kids need a place to call home until they can either be reunified with their parents or placed in an adoptive family.

It isn't easy to care for a troubled child or deal with the social service system. You give your heart with no guarantees—but isn't that like Jesus' love?

If you simply can't open your home to a foster child, find a foster family and offer to help. Be their biggest fan and advocate. Together you can give a child a future and hope.

Lord, fostering a child is a huge commitment—
but please show me how I might become involved.

Friday

CONSIDER ADOPTION

*Religion that God our Father accepts as pure
and faultless is this: to look after orphans
and widows in their distress and to keep
oneself from being polluted by the world.*
JAMES 1:27 NIV

David and I had always considered growing our family through adoption. After our two foster girls were reunited with their birth mom, we prayerfully and carefully reevaluated our adoption plans. Did we still want to adopt? Yes, absolutely. Were we ready to pursue adoption at that point? No—we waited until our biological children were a bit older.

Adoption is part of our family's experience. Our daughter and son-in-law adopted Nathan at birth and have a strong relationship with his birth mother. Other family members have adopted children from orphanages overseas or within the extended family.

When you adopt, you're committing your whole life to a particular child, no matter what. When adoptive children have experienced trauma, raising them probably won't look the same as raising birth children. Adoptive parents need every resource and helper they can get.

In the United States, the average age of children needing an adoptive home is six. Might God be nudging you to consider giving one of them a home?

*Lord, this is a huge question, but You are far bigger.
Guide me in Your perfect way, for Your own glory.*

Date: _____

Lord, stretch me outside my comfort zones so that I depend on You more than ever. Show me the hard things You want me to do—things that will add amazing highlights in my life.

5 TOPICS COVERED THIS WEEK:

Monday: visit a missionary overseas
Tuesday: host a refugee couple
Wednesday: sponsor a needy child
Thursday: serve as a foster parent
Friday: consider adoption

3 WAYS GIVING SACRIFICIALLY BLESSES ME:

1. ....

2. ....

3. ....

3 WAYS GIVING SACRIFICIALLY WORRIES ME:

1. ....

2. ....

3. ....

How I want to respond to these truths:

....

....

....

....

....

....

....

....

....

....

....

LORD, HERE'S WHAT'S GOING ON IN MY LIFE RIGHT NOW. . .

OTHER THINGS I NEED TO
SHARE WITH YOU, LORD. . .

Lord, when it comes to this
new life map, I need to. . .

But [God Almighty]
knows the way that I take;
when he has tested me,
I will come forth as gold.
JOB 23:10 NIV

Thank You, Lord, for
hearing my prayers
and for helping
me take action!
AMEN.

WEEK 26
Finishing Well, Part 1

Billy Graham. What a life! What a legacy! Yet Billy Graham made it clear in the early 1980s that his ministry could be over in a moment. "If I should ever take any glory away from God," he said, "God would take His hand off my life and my lips would turn to clay." It's a sobering thought that the Lord could nullify what any given individual does best.

Renowned research professor J. Robert Clinton has invested much of his career analyzing why people do—or don't—finish well. He once did a comparative study of the lives of more than eight hundred Christian leaders, concluding that, "Few leaders finish well."

Clinton lists six barriers to finishing well, including unresolved sin. This week, we'll look at the other five barriers: (1) the misuse of money; (2) the abuse of power; (3) unchecked pride; (4) illicit sexual relationships; and (5) unresolved family problems.

We'll consider biblical truths to keep us safe and productive throughout life.

> *Let us not become weary in doing good, for at the proper time we will reap a harvest if we do not give up.*
> GALATIANS 6:9 NIV

Monday

THE MISUSE OF MONEY

He [Judas Iscariot] was a thief; as keeper of the money
bag, he used to help himself to what was put into it.
JOHN 12:6 NIV

From the first time he "borrowed" a little money from the apostles' fund to the moment he pocketed thirty pieces of silver (Matthew 26:14–16), Judas was looking out for his own interests.

When he objected to a woman's lavish pouring of perfume on Jesus, it wasn't because Judas cared about the poor. What Jesus saw as an act of worship, Judas calculated as a loss of funds to pilfer (John 12:1–6). With ease, Satan entered Judas' heart, propelling him to cut a deal with the leading priests to betray Jesus (Luke 22:1–6).

Even when Judas was later filled with remorse, he never turned back to God in repentance. He simply regretted the tragic turn of events and took what appeared to be the easiest way out: suicide (Matthew 27:5).

Scripture warns strongly against the idea of following the Lord as a means to financial gain (1 Peter 1:13–19; 2 Peter 2:1–16). However Judas began with Jesus, he ended very poorly. Let's value our Lord far above wealth—for who He is, not for what He might give us.

Lord, I want to value You far above all other
things. Warn me in those moments that I stray.

Tuesday

THE ABUSE OF POWER

Then Absalom sent secret messengers
throughout the tribes of Israel to say,
"As soon as you hear the sound of the trumpets,
then say, 'Absalom is king in Hebron.'"

2 SAMUEL 15:10 NIV

In many ways, Absalom was the perfect politician. Then again, Absalom pursued what he wanted all the wrong ways—for all the wrong reasons. He kept going his way, not God's, to right the supposed wrongs in his life and to gain the power he thought he deserved.

In his desire to be king, Absalom looked not to God's will, but to his own. He decided that he alone should call all the shots—and plotted to take the kingdom of Israel by cunning and force. Even if that meant destroying his father, King David.

Absalom had what it took to be a national leader—political sense, excellent counsel, leadership skills, even good looks. Yet he grabbed at personal power rather than seeking God's best. And the hand that grabbed for more and more came up empty.

It is only when our hands are open before God, seeking His glory, that He can fill them with blessing and power.

Lord, I want to seek Your will far above my own.
Stop me if I ever try to abuse earthly power.

UNCHECKED PRIDE

> Asa was angry with the seer because of this;
> he was so enraged that he put him in prison. At the
> same time Asa brutally oppressed some of the people.
> 2 CHRONICLES 16:10 NIV

Asa was a "white sheep" of the family—the godly son of wicked parents. From the beginning of his kingship, he determined to reign differently from his father, Abijah. Asa set his course to seek the Lord, and God overwhelmingly blessed him for it.

Unfortunately, when Asa was old, his will became his own. He looked to human resources to rescue him from enemies, and then bristled when confronted. In pride, he kept looking to human help alone, even for his physical well-being. He died without calling to the Lord even once. How tragic!

If Asa had died only a few years earlier, he would have been known as one of Judah's greatest kings. Instead, he finished abysmally. Asa's failed life should prompt each of us to ask, "When I am old, will I still look for God's divine help at every step? Or will I have developed my own way of handling life?"

What are you doing to walk humbly with God now? Both Peter and James remind us that God opposes the proud but gives grace to the humble.

Lord, I want to repent of unchecked pride
in my life. I acknowledge You as the
King of my life, now and forever.

Thursday

ILLICIT SEXUAL RELATIONSHIPS

> One day Samson went to Gaza, where he saw a
> prostitute. He went in to spend the night with her.
> JUDGES 16:1 NIV

The account of Samson covers more chapters in the book of Judges than any other character. The stories tell of Samson's supernaturally foretold birth, the Lord's blessing on his childhood, his lifelong Nazirite vow, the Spirit's hold on his life, his incredible strength and his unbridled passions and lusts.

Samson's story is tragically short. One can only imagine how much more he could have done for the Lord. If Samson hadn't been ruined by his passions and lusts, perhaps an entire book of the Bible would have been written about him!

Like Samson, you and I have a life story to write. And like Samson, we have important choices to make. Samson mistakenly thought he was strong enough to bear the growing weight of his sexual sins. It's a burden that crushed the strongest man in the world.

The misuse of sexuality isn't just a man's sin. Satan would love to see it crush us too. Flee youthful lusts (2 Peter 2:22 NKJV), but know that if you stumble, Jesus offers forgiveness and newness to every woman who asks (see John 8:1–11).

*Lord, J don't want to be ruled by passions
and lusts. Help me to acknowledge You as
sovereign over every area of my life.*

Friday

UNRESOLVED FAMILY PROBLEMS

"No, my sons;" [Eli said,] "the report I hear
spreading among the LORD's people is not good."
1 SAMUEL 2:24 NIV

In spite of his priestly duties and privileges, Eli had put his own family's interests ahead of the Lord's. It seems Eli's affections were set on the prosperity to be gained from the tabernacle offerings. And he preferred to keep the peace rather than deal with deep issues in his home.

Years before, Eli's forefather Phineas had brandished a sword to protect the nation from gross immorality (Numbers 25:1–13). Eli weakly protested his sons' open immorality and theft committed within the Lord's tabernacle. He barely cared when God warned him, and his family paid a terrible price.

Unlike Eli, Abigail was a woman who took radical action to both honor the Lord and protect her family from sin and punishment. She acted wisely, in faith, instead of allowing her abusive husband to ruin their home (1 Samuel 25:3–30).

The Bible honestly records the sins and problems that run through even godly families. Instead of despairing, we can seek God's grace and obey Him in making hard choices and changes. When we do, we will bless generations to come.

Lord, please help me to act boldly out of a deep
passion for Your holiness, glory, and honor.

Date:

Lord, it's sobering to think that You could nullify my life, work, and legacy in an instant—if I disregard the examples of those who have gone before me.

5 TOPICS COVERED THIS WEEK:

Monday: the misuse of money
Tuesday: the abuse of power
Wednesday: unchecked pride
Thursday: illicit sexual relationships
Friday: unresolved family problems

3 WAYS I THINK I'M FINISHING WELL:

1.
2.
3.

3 WAYS I NEED TO BE CAREFUL:

1.
2.
3.

How I want to respond to these truths:

LORD, HERE'S WHAT'S GOING ON IN MY LIFE RIGHT NOW. . .

OTHER THINGS I NEED TO
SHARE WITH YOU, LORD. . .

Lord, when it comes to this
new life map, I need to. . .

Doing wrong is like a joke
to a fool, but wisdom
is pleasure to a man
of understanding.
PROVERBS 10:23 ESV

Thank You, Lord, for
hearing my prayers
and for helping
me take action!
AMEN.

WEEK 27
Finishing Well, Part 2

Last week, we looked at the obstacles to living (and finishing) life well. Thankfully, J. Robert Clinton has identified five things that help people finish well: (1) a lifetime perspective on living for and serving God; (2) fresh encounters with God; (3) personal daily disciplines; (4) a lifelong learning posture; and (5) lifelong mentoring by a number of people.

While we each can think of people who've crashed their lives, we also can look to women like Amy Carmichael, Mother Teresa, Corrie ten Boom, Elisabeth Elliot, Ruth Bell Graham, and many others who truly finished well. You probably interact with some of these women each week—maybe even call them "mom."

May you also be a woman who lives your whole life for God— to the very end!

> *The time for my departure is near. I have fought the good fight, I have finished the race, I have kept the faith.*
>
> 2 TIMOTHY 4:6–7 NIV

Monday

SERVE GOD YOUR WHOLE LIFE

*[Anna] came along just as Simeon was talking
with Mary and Joseph, and she began praising God.
She talked about the child to everyone who had been
waiting expectantly for God to rescue Jerusalem.*
LUKE 2:38 NLT

God had promised the priest Simeon that he would not die until he saw the Messiah. Even with no such guarantee, Anna too eagerly awaited the Messiah's appearance (Daniel 9:20–25). While these two devout people waited, they lived righteously, walking with God in obedience and worshipping Him with all their hearts.

As Mary and Joseph entered the temple with baby Jesus cradled in their arms, they looked like any other faithful couple fulfilling their duty to God. But to an old man and an old woman led by the Holy Spirit, this little family stood out like a beacon. The small child and His parents were welcomed to God's house as no family had ever been greeted before.

Anna's commitment to serve God carried her from young widowhood to the climactic experience of her old age—meeting the Messiah. When we finish our lives, you and I will have that same joy of meeting Jesus face to face.

*Lord, I want to serve You my whole life long.
May I be as faithful as Simeon and Anna.*

Tuesday

HEART OPEN TO GOD ENCOUNTERS

"Do not be afraid, Mary;
you have found favor with God."
LUKE 1:30 NIV

When the angel approached Mary with a proclamation that she would become pregnant, her first question was a real one: "How will this be?" (Luke 1:34). Nothing like this had happened before! The angel assured Mary that the Holy Spirit would conceive God's Son, then gave her news of the barren Elizabeth's pregnancy. Mary immediately answered with full acceptance: "I am the Lord's servant May your word to me be fulfilled" (Luke 1:38). God visited the woman whose heart was already open to Him.

For his part, Joseph believed what the Lord revealed to him in a series of vivid dreams. Each time, Joseph quickly translated his belief into action at great personal cost. He never hesitated to follow God's leading.

Like Mary and Joseph, we can live each day expectantly, open to God's voice. With the Holy Spirit living within us, our encounters with God can happen at any moment. The question is, are you willing to respond to what the Lord reveals, no matter the cost?

Lord, I want to experience fresh encounters with You.
Please keep my heart open to You at every turn.

Wednesday

DAILY DEDICATED AND DISCIPLINED

Don't let anyone look down on you because you are young, but set an example for the believers in speech, in conduct, in love, in faith and in purity.
1 TIMOTHY 4:12 NIV

Timothy was young enough to have his ministry questioned. But he was also mature enough in his faith to be entrusted with the spiritual leadership of the church in a rather large city.

Although Timothy's father apparently was not a Christian, his Jewish mother and grandmother had saturated his young heart and mind with the holy scriptures (2 Timothy 1:5, 3:15). By the time he met Paul, Timothy was ready to convert his well-rounded biblical knowledge into active service for the Lord (Acts 16:1–4).

When Timothy was commissioned, Paul and the elders at his church laid their hands on him and publicly prophesied that the Lord had uniquely equipped him to minister to others (1 Timothy 4:14; 2 Timothy 1:6). After that, Timothy traveled with the apostle and his evangelistic team for at least a year and a half (Acts 16:1–18:19).

Paul valued Timothy for his dedicated heart and soul—his love for God's people and his commitment to stay at the work of serving them. How will you and I show our dedication to the Lord today?

Lord, may I be daily dedicated and disciplined to follow You.

Thursday

COMMITTED TO LIFELONG LEARNING

[Apollos] began to speak boldly in the synagogue.
When Priscilla and Aquila heard him,
they invited him to their home and explained
to him the way of God more adequately.
ACTS 18:26 NIV

A hardworking, blue-collar Italian couple approached a young, eloquent Egyptian scholar. Would he care to come over for supper? Along with the meal, they served up more of what the preacher wanted most—further truth about God and His Son, Jesus Christ.

As brilliant as he was, Apollos had not yet heard the whole message of the gospel. Like someone who has read the first two books of a trilogy, he needed to learn the exciting conclusion. Priscilla and Aquila gave Apollos wonderful news: there was more to believing in Jesus as Messiah. To show one's desire to be right with God, there was more than simply following John's baptism. There was a personal acceptance of Jesus' life and work, a gaining of salvation!

Despite his impressive credentials, Apollos never assumed he knew it all. He humbled himself and his ministry grew accordingly. Apollos is a stellar example of a Christian committed to lifelong learning. Are you?

Lord, please make me a lifelong learner.
Thank You for what I'm learning right now.

Friday
MULTIPLE MENTORS FOR LIFE

The reason I left you in Crete was that you
might put in order what was left unfinished and
appoint elders in every town, as I directed you.
TITUS 1:5 NIV

"Multiple mentors, you say? I can't even find one!" Maybe you need to rethink the concept of a mentor. It can be any person who influences your life.

As one of Paul's coworkers, Titus must have accumulated quite a few Empire Express mileage points. Each time we read about Titus, Paul was sending him on another mission trip around the Mediterranean. Titus actively ministered among the Corinthian believers. Later, Paul asked Titus to minister on the island of Crete, and a short time after that, Paul directed Titus to Nicopolis. In each of these cities, Titus served alongside the believers, becoming even more of a leader at the same time.

Before all of this, Paul had taken Titus to the Jerusalem Council (Acts 15:2; Galatians 2:3). There Titus had the opportunity to be mentored not just by Paul, but by Barnabas, Peter, James, and others.

No matter how much life and ministry experience we accumulate, we always benefit from mentors in our lives. Do you have a mentor right now? If not, who might you approach?

*Lord, please help me to recognize and thank
my mentors—past, present, and future.*

Date: ....

Lord, I love to see the radiant smile of a woman who's lived her entire life for You. May I be among their number!

5 TOPICS COVERED THIS WEEK:

Monday: serve God your whole life
Tuesday: heart open to God encounters
Wednesday: daily dedicated and disciplined
Thursday: committed to lifelong learning
Friday: multiple mentors for life

3 WAYS LIVING FAITHFULLY EXCITES ME:

1. ....

2. ....

3. ....

3 WAYS LIVING FAITHFULLY CHALLENGES ME:

1. ....

2. ....

3. ....

How I want to respond to these truths:

....

....

....

....

....

....

....

....

....

....

LORD, HERE'S WHAT'S GOING ON IN MY LIFE RIGHT NOW. . .

OTHER THINGS I NEED TO
SHARE WITH YOU, LORD. . .

Lord, when it comes to this
new life map, I need to. . .

Listen to advice and
accept discipline, and
at the end you will be
counted among the wise.
PROVERBS 19:20 NIV

Thank You, Lord, for
hearing my prayers
and for helping
me take action!
AMEN.

WEEK 28
Knowing God

You might think the most important question in life is, "Who am I?" It's not. No other question is more crucial to answer than, "Who is God?"

Get this one right—and experience who He is each day—and the world and life gain meaning, purpose, and joy. One mentor said, "I am convinced that the answers to every problem and issue of life for both time and eternity are resolved through a correct understanding of God." What hope! The opposite? In the words of a respected teacher, "When I don't take time to reflect on the God I serve, He becomes too small to help me; so I decide to handle the anxiety myself and blame God for it later."

So then, "Who is God?" We will spend eternity learning this answer. But we can begin now with who God reveals Himself to be in His Word. Myriads of biblical and theological words describe God; we'll explore five this week.

> "Yours, LORD, is the greatness and the power and
> the glory and the majesty and the splendor,
> for everything in heaven and earth is yours."
>
> 1 CHRONICLES 29:11 NIV

Monday

GOD'S AWE INSPIRING SOVEREIGNTY

*"Sovereign Lord. . .you made the heavens and the
earth and the sea, and everything in them."*
ACTS 4:24 NIV

The term sovereign appears hundreds of times in scripture, and it's embedded more than sixty-seven hundred times in the sacred divine name YHWH. The latter typically appears as the word LORD—capitalized that way in most modern translations of the Old Testament.

When we think about who God is, we begin by describing Him as all-powerful (omnipotent) and present everywhere (omnipresent). Biblical heroes rejoiced over both of these aspects.

King David said, "The LORD has established his throne in heaven, and his kingdom rules over all" (Psalm 103:19 NIV). Paul described God as "the blessed and only Ruler, the King of kings and Lord of lords, who alone is immortal and who lives in unapproachable light, whom no one has seen or can see. To him be honor and might forever. Amen" (1 Timothy 6:15–16 NIV).

God's power and presence permeate every millisecond and millimeter of existence. Do you recognize it in your life? When you do, you rest in the fact that God is not caught off guard by world events or personal problems. You live with confidence that He is on the throne—and you are not alone.

*Lord, I thank You for Your sovereignty in my
life. You are all-powerful and with me always.
To know that is awe-inspiring, indeed!*

Tuesday
GOD'S PURPOSEFUL PROVIDENCE

*"You gave me life and showed me kindness,
and in your providence watched over my spirit."*
JOB 10:12 NIV

In answering the question "Who is God?" four of this week's terms appear throughout the Bible. The word *providence*, however, does not. The term appears in the last sentence of the Declaration of Independence, and in thousands of other works published over the past 450 years. Yet during that period *providence* doesn't appear once in the vast majority of English Bible translations. Job 10:12 in the New International Version is a rare exception.

So is God's providence an idea we bring to the Bible, or is it intrinsic to scripture? Stories about Abraham, Joseph, Ruth, David, Ezra, Esther, and other heroes of the faith clearly demonstrate God's (mostly) invisible hand at work, purposefully guiding His people and providing for their needs.

More importantly, the Lord repeatedly declares His purposeful providence. He assured Isaiah: "I make known the end from the beginning, from ancient times, what is still to come I say, 'My purpose will stand, and I will do all that I please'" (Isaiah 46:10 NIV).

So does God's purposeful guidance and goodness permeate your life? Yes! Life is abundant when you recognize and rejoice in both.

*Lord, I thank You for Your providence in my
life. Help me to recognize it at every turn.*

Wednesday

GOD'S GLORIOUS HOLINESS

Therefore, since we have these promises,
dear friends, let us purify ourselves from
everything that contaminates body and spirit,
perfecting holiness out of reverence for God.
2 CORINTHIANS 7:1 NIV

Holy and its synonyms appear more than sixteen hundred times throughout the Bible. It quickly becomes clear that God is holy, people aren't, God expects us to be holy, and we can't be without His divine transformation.

The Lord told His people: "Do not profane my holy name, for I must be acknowledged as holy" (Leviticus 22:32 NIV). He also said, "Be holy because I, the LORD your God, am holy" (Leviticus 19:2 NIV).

Biblical heroes felt the dichotomies of holiness, which both challenged them and spurred their faith into action. In the middle of the Bible we're told, "Worship the Lord in the splendor of his holiness; tremble before him, all the earth" (Psalm 96:9 NIV). Toward the end of the Bible we're told, "God disciplines us for our good, in order that we may share in his holiness" (Hebrews 12:10 NIV).

So does God's glory and purity permeate your life? Yes! Now is the time to confess any known sins and embrace God's holiness anew.

Lord, I thank You for Your holiness in my
life. Show me the sins I need to confess, and
help me to gladly embrace Your holiness.

Thursday

GOD'S GRACIOUS LOVE

*God's love has been poured out into our hearts
through the Holy Spirit, who has been given to us.*
ROMANS 5:5 NIV

Jesus and His apostles didn't "invent" the idea of God's love. Far from it!

Remember the Lord's sacred name, YHWH? Here's the first part of how God Himself defines it: "The LORD, the LORD, the compassionate and gracious God, slow to anger, abounding in love and faithfulness, maintaining love to thousands, and forgiving wickedness, rebellion and sin" (Exodus 34:5–7 NIV).

Did you notice the word *love* appears twice in that statement?

Actually, the terms *God* and *love* appear adjacent to each other many times throughout the Bible, especially in the New Testament. The most famous of those verses is John 3:16. Other famous verses about God's love include Romans 5:5 (quoted above), Romans 5:8, and Romans 8:38–39. Still others include 1 John 4:7–10, 1 John 4:16, and 1 John 4:19.

But it's not enough to simply know *about* God's love. It is to be experienced through the time and trust we give Him.

So does God's graciousness and passion permeate your life? Yes! Open your heart to receive that divine love right now.

*Lord, I thank You for Your love in my heart. Help me
to experience Your love afresh and anew today.*

Friday

GOD'S HEAVENLY MYSTERY

"For my thoughts are not your thoughts,
neither are your ways my ways," declares the LORD.
ISAIAH 55:8 NIV

When we discuss who God is, we can't overlook the fact that He is all-knowing (omniscient). This doesn't just mean God knows all the facts in the universe. Though that's true, God knows much, much more!

Remember phone books? They contained thousands of facts, but none that could change your life. By themselves, facts are stupid. God not only possesses all knowledge, but all discernment, all insight, all understanding, all wisdom and super-high-above-our-heads ways.

He Himself put it this way: "As the heavens are higher than the earth, so are my ways higher than your ways and my thoughts than your thoughts" (Isaiah 55:9 NIV).

In other words, "God alone knows," multiplied by eternity and infinity. None of us knows a millionth of one percent of everything that's true and right and important and life changing. So why in the world are we tempted to think we know better than God? Not a chance!

Does God's higher, heavenly wisdom and way permeate your life? Yes! Humbly acknowledge His mystery today.

Lord, I'm grateful that Your mystery permeates
my life. I gladly affirm that You know
best how to run my life. Please do so!

Date: _____

Lord, I want to know You as much as a human being can know the Creator of all. Thank You for placing delightful reminders of who You are throughout the Bible. May I never forget them!

5 TOPICS COVERED THIS WEEK:

Monday: God's awe-inspiring sovereignty

Tuesday: God's purposeful providence

Wednesday: God's glorious holiness

Thursday: God's gracious love

Friday: God's heavenly mystery

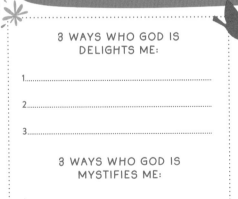

3 WAYS WHO GOD IS DELIGHTS ME:

1. ....

2. ....

3. ....

3 WAYS WHO GOD IS MYSTIFIES ME:

1. ....

2. ....

3. ....

How I want to respond to these truths:

....

....

....

....

....

....

....

....

....

....

....

LORD, HERE'S WHAT'S GOING ON IN MY LIFE RIGHT NOW...

OTHER THINGS I NEED TO
SHARE WITH YOU, LORD...

Lord, when it comes to this
new life map, I need to. . .

"For Yours is the kingdom
and the power and
the glory forever."
MATTHEW 6:13 NKJV

Thank You, Lord, for
hearing my prayers
and for helping
me take action!
AMEN.

Scripture Index

GENESIS

1:26 10
1:27 71
2:7 10
2:24 64
3:15 12
9 162
18:1 163
45 42

EXODUS

16:23 133
32:25 139
34:5–7 228
40:16 103

LEVITICUS

19:2 227
22:32 227

NUMBERS

25:1–13 213

DEUTERONOMY

6:6–7 .... 75, 164
8:18 178
10:12–13 89
10:18 85
31:8 170

JOSHUA

1:8 48
24:15 72

JUDGES

16:1 212

RUTH

2:7 163

1 SAMUEL

2:24 213
14 101
16:7 121
17:45–47 51
25:3–30 213

2 SAMUEL

11 44
15:10 210

1 KINGS

10:1 115
19:6 163

1 CHRONICLES

29:11 224

2 CHRONICLES

16:10 211
16:12 24

NEHEMIAH

8:8 42

JOB

1:21 108
1:22 108
10:12 226

23:10 207
23:12 41
28:28 155

PSALMS
1:2 .... 52, 145
1:2–3 152
3:5 131
23:1–6 90
23:2–3 168
25:12 111
32:8 169
34:3 43
34:18 28
37:23 171
42:11 114
51 44
63:6 145
68:5 79
77:12 145
82:3 203
90:17 121
96:9 227
100:4 28
103:13–14 141
103:19 225
104:24 137
111:10 155
119:11 45
119:15 145
119:16 88
119:18 47
119:105 53

121:8 173
127:2 132
127:3 .... 74, 106
139:23–24 27
142:1–2 26
143:5 145
143:8 67
147:5 20

PROVERBS
1:7 155
2:5 155
2:11 148
3:1–4 120
3:3 68
4:23 149
8:34–35 7
9:9–11 40
9:10 155
10:22 184
10:23 215
13:10 185
13:11 176
16:9 175
18:24 77
19:20 223
22:7 187
31:29 113

ECCLESIASTES
3:1 136
7:12 186
9:10 122
12:12–14 155

ISAIAH

1:17 204
7:10–14 24
26:3 129
30:15 128
46:10 226
49:23 29
55:8 229
55:9 229

DANIEL

9:20–25 217

MICAH

6:8 96

MALACHI

3:10 200

MATTHEW

4:4 44
4:19 17
5:16 125
6:9–10 97
6:10 104
6:13 231
6:21 191
6:33 98
7:7 31
9:10 80
10:42 161
11:28 .... 123, 130
26:14–16 209
27:5 209
28:20 56

MARK

4:38 163
6:31 138
9:37 76
10:51 24
12:31 116

LUKE

1:34 218
1:38 218
2:38 217
8:3 197
10:8 162
10:41 81
12:15 188
14:13 84
14:28 180
16:14 176
22:1–6 209

JOHN

3:16 .... 11, 228
3:16–18 91
4:10 161
8:1–11 212
10:10 .... 12, 143
12:1–6 209
12:6 209
15 60
15:1–8 153
15:5 95
16:27 25

ACTS

4:24 225

9:31 60
15:2 221
16:1–4 219
16:15 83
16:34 82
17:28 146
18:26 220
20:33–34 181
20:35 .... 179, 192, 196
21:8 201
26:18 16
28:7 202

ROMANS

1:17 23
5:5 228
5:8 228
8:6 145
8:28 99
8:38–39 228
10:9–10 92
10:17 43
12:1–2 20
12:2 109
12:5 57
12:11 192
12:19 147
13:8 65
14 146
15:4 51
15:13 135

1 CORINTHIANS

2:16 145

3:7 153
7:28 105
9:24 146
9:25 165
9:26 146
10:31 144
12:26 60
13:7 66
15:10 112
15:58 193

2 CORINTHIANS

4:17............................ 13
7:1.............................. 227
9:7 195
9:8........................... 189
10:5..................... 20, 147

GALATIANS

2:2 146
2:3 221
5:7 146
6:9............................208

EPHESIANS

4:17...........................145
6:2–3 73
6:18 37
6:19............................ 35

PHILIPPIANS

2:13...........................157
3:14............................159
4:4 28
4:6–7 93

4:8......................145, 149
4:9........................ 119
4:11 176
4:12...........................176
4:18 197
4:19 199

Colossians
1:3–4......................... 32
1:10 155
1:16 115
3:8 117
3:14...........................64
3:23–24 7

1 Thessalonians
4:11 177
4:11–12 167

2 Thessalonians
1:3...........................154
1:11...................18, 33, 34

1 Timothy
2:1 39
2:1–2 36
3:1–7 194
3:15 56
4:4–5 162
4:8........................ 160
4:12.........................219
4:14.........................219
5:23 50
6:6........................... 182
6:10–11 50

6:12............................ 13
6:15–16..................... 225
6:17........................... 151

2 Timothy
1:5............................219
1:6 219
1:7...........................127
3:15.........................219
3:16–17 .... 21, 50
4:2 58
4:6–7 216

Titus
1:5...........................221
1:5–9 194

Hebrews
4:12.......................33, 49
9:27 20
10:24–25 61
10:36........................ 100
11:1................................8
11:3 9
11:6 15
12:10 227
13:5...........................183
13:16 87
13:17...........................59
13:20–21.....................101

James
1:17 140
1:22...........................55
1:25...........................52

1:27 205
4:15 107

1 PETER

1:7 13
1:13–19 209
1:21 17
1:22 28
2:9 63
2:21 51
4:8 69
5:1–4 194

2 PETER

2:1–16 209
2:22 212
3:9 91
3:18 156

1 JOHN

4:7–10 228
4:16 228
4:19 228

ANOTHER POWERFUL DEVOTIONAL
FROM BARBOUR PUBLISHING

The heavenly Creator is with you and for you. And when you're doing life with Him, you have the gifts of His abundant light and grace. He gives you the strength you need to keep on going. . .to push through hard things and come out on the other side, a victorious woman of God! These 180 empowering devotions and prayers will remind you that you're never alone and always loved. With God by your side, you can do hard things!

Hardcover / ISBN 978-1-63609-956-9